Praise for *Meditation: Coming to Know Your Mind*

"Meditation: Coming to Know Your Mind offers a wonderful guide for anyone aiming to practice mindfulness leading to wisdom and a more meaningful, happier life. Matteo's direct approach makes the book easy to read, while his thoroughness gives the reader a clear understanding of the various techniques and methods available. It's an excellent resource for anyone wishing to learn the practice of meditation or for a more experienced practitioner seeking renewed inspiration and understanding."

<small>SHARON SALZBERG, AUTHOR OF *REAL HAPPINESS* AND *REAL LOVE*</small>

"Meditation: Coming to Know Your Mind is a wonderfully refreshing, well-informed, and practical guide to a rich array of meditative practices drawn from the Tibetan Buddhist tradition. The practices explained here, interspersed with illuminating personal narratives, are central to Buddhism and are at the same time relevant to everyone seeking a more mindful, empathetic, meaningful way of life. I recommend it to beginners and seasoned meditators alike."

<small>B. ALAN WALLACE, PRESIDENT, SANTA BARBARA INSTITUTE FOR CONSCIOUSNESS STUDIES</small>

"A clear, accessible, reliable, and inspiring guide to meditation that will prove very helpful for those who aspire to train their mind and become a better person."

<small>MATTHIEU RICARD, AUTHOR OF *WHY MEDITATE?* AND *ALTRUISM*</small>

"I have long been searching for a clear, compassionate guide to meditation that I can recommend to people from all walks of life. Matteo Pistono's Meditation: Coming to Know Your Mind *is the clearest and most insightful guide anybody could wish for, whether beginner or seasoned practitioner. While grounded in the Buddhist tradition,* Meditation *is a real treasure for anybody who seeks to explore this ancient wisdom practice in a modern setting. A brilliant beacon of light on the path to mindfulness!"*

<small>MICHAELA HAAS, PHD, AUTHOR OF *DAKINI POWER* AND *BOUNCING FORWARD*</small>

Meditation

Made Easy

Meditation

Made Easy

Coming to Know Your Mind

Matteo Pistono

HAY HOUSE

Carlsbad, California • New York City
London • Sydney • New Delhi

Published in the United Kingdom by:
Hay House UK Ltd, Astley House, 33 Notting Hill Gate, London W11 3JQ
Tel: +44 (0)20 3675 2450; Fax: +44 (0)20 3675 2451; www.hayhouse.co.uk

Published in the United States of America by:
Hay House Inc., PO Box 5100, Carlsbad, CA 92018-5100
Tel: (1) 760 431 7695 or (800) 654 5126
Fax: (1) 760 431 6948 or (800) 650 5115; www.hayhouse.com

Published in Australia by:
Hay House Australia Ltd, 18/36 Ralph St, Alexandria NSW 2015
Tel: (61) 2 9669 4299; Fax: (61) 2 9669 4144; www.hayhouse.com.au

Published in India by:
Hay House Publishers India, Muskaan Complex, Plot No.3, B-2,
Vasant Kunj, New Delhi 110 070
Tel: (91) 11 4176 1620; Fax: (91) 11 4176 1630; www.hayhouse.co.in

This book was previously published under the title *Meditation*
(*Hay House Basics* series); ISBN: 978-1-78180-862-7

A catalogue record for this book is available from the British Library.

ISBN: 978-1-78817-244-8
Ebook ISBN: 978-1-78817-251-6

Interior images: lotus flower, Minette Mangahas; author
photo, Hay House; all other images Matteo Pistono

Printed and bound by CPI Group (UK) Ltd, Croydon, CR0 4YY

For my brother, and community of meditators
in Washington, DC, London, Goa, and beyond.

May our journey of meditation reveal
the teacher within each of us.

Contents

List of Practices and Guided Meditations   xiii

Introduction   xv

Chapter 1: An Auspicious Beginning   1

   Why meditate?   3

   Cultivating the mind   4

   A meditator's toolbox   6

   Where to begin?   9

   "Good in the beginning"   12

Chapter 2: Cultivating Stillness and Comfort   17

   Connecting body and mind through body scanning   18

   Alertness in our meditation posture   23

   The breath, our companion on the path of
   meditation   34

   What to do with all of these thoughts?   39

   Being kind to ourselves   43

   Eight tips for establishing a daily meditation
   practice   45

Chapter 3: Discerning Reality   **51**

Focusing on the present moment   52

Stillness, silence, and awareness   56

Attention, vigilance, and spaciousness   58

Mindfulness is only part of the story   60

Chapter 4: Opening Completely to Our World   **67**

The objects of our five senses   68

What is awareness?   74

Transforming distraction into meditation   78

How to deal with strong emotions and
'experiences' during meditation   85

"What if I feel bodily pain when I meditate?"   89

Caution! How not to become an escape artist
from your life   92

Chapter 5: Integrating Meditation into Everyday Life   **95**

Develop an interest in meditation   95

The spontaneous and informal session   97

Walking meditation   99

Falling asleep   103

Drinking and eating like the Buddha   106

Chapter 6: Working within Our Mind   **113**

A map of distraction: the Eight Consciousnesses   120

The Dalai Lama's sandals   128

Advice on gaining flexibility, stability, and
ease in your meditation posture   131

Chapter 7: Meditation, Contemplation, and Thinking   **135**

    Complementary practices   136

    Expanding into the ever-changing present   139

    Go outside!   144

    Finding space in life   148

Chapter 8: Focus, Friends, and Teachers   **155**

    Focus   155

    Spiritual friends   156

    Teachers   157

Make a Plan for Your Meditation Practice   **161**

    Consistency is the key   163

    The ripple effect   165

Further Reading   167

Index   169

About the Author   177

List of Practices and Guided Meditations

Practices

Motivation and dedication	14
Letting go before sleeping	105

Guided meditations

Body scanning	30
Discovering the breath	36
The breath as our companion	54
Relaxed and alert with the breath	63
Sound	71
All five senses	82
Walking	101
Drinking tea	108
Eating	110
Mind	117
Spacious out-breath	141
Resting in the space between thoughts	150

Introduction

Twenty-five years ago I traveled to northern India. It was the first of many pilgrimages I would undertake in the Himalayas. On my initial sojourn I met a meditation master who lived as a hermit in a cave. He'd been meditating there for over 40 years. His eyes were filled with kindness and a vast spaciousness like the sky above the mountains.

I was a frustrated activist at the time. I didn't have the patience to remain in America and work within the political system. I blamed the power structure for the many injustices I saw around me. But I was angrier with myself for not being able to enact the change that I wanted to see in politics and in society. I was seeking some kind of refuge in the Himalayas, if only from the tightly bound tension in my own heart and mind.

When I met the meditation master, I asked him, "How can I help change the world for the better?"

He told me, "First, you need to learn to meditate—only then will you know yourself."

I wasn't sure how that would help.

"Only after truly knowing yourself," he said, "will you really be able to help others."

I didn't know how to start meditating. But that day I vowed to learn.

The last thing the meditation master told me before I left his cave was, "You have to taste meditation. You have to do it. It's not enough to know about it. You can have lots of knowledge and read many books about meditation but unless you practice it, it won't be of any use to you."

I began studying with various Tibetan Buddhist meditation masters and then lived in Tibet and Nepal for about a decade. It was during this period that I met my principal meditation teacher just outside Kathmandu Valley. He was an accomplished scholar-meditator and served as the abbot of a small hermitage. He lived a very simple life and felt my gifts of maple syrup from America and Swiss cough drops were decadent! I entered into the traditional teacher–student relationship with him and for years he guided me through various meditation texts and commentaries.

He continually checked my learning and experience, oftentimes pointing out my misunderstandings. When

I wanted to jump ahead in the step-by-step meditation instructions, he would say something like, "Enthusiasm is as strong as a horse, but as short as a sheep's tail," and then counsel me to be steadfast and consistent. To this day I continue to follow his meditation instructions and study his teachings.

During this time in Nepal I also practiced intensively S.N. Goenka's Vipassana meditation teachings, first in group retreats and thereafter as a daily practice.

In between living in Asia and America, I received a master's in Indian philosophy from the University of London and trained in modern yoga postures and especially *pranayama*—yogic breathing practices. I wrote several books about my travels among meditation masters in Asia, including *In the Shadow of the Buddha: One Man's Journey of Spiritual Discovery in Tibet*, *Fearless in Tibet: The Life of the Mystic Tertön Sogyal*, and *Roar: Sulak Sivaraksa and the Path of Socially Engaged Buddhism*.

While I've had the great fortune of training and practicing different techniques with great yogis and masters from various spiritual traditions, I've always returned to the fundamental practice of meditation as my rock, my refuge, my daily sustenance. Meditation nourishes contentment in my life. This is why I've written this book: to share the essence of meditation practice, with the aspiration that you and others may be empowered and find refuge within yourself—find solace within your own heart and mind.

This life we have is precious. And indeed, it goes by so quickly. Let's not miss the chance to find the true source of contentment within ourselves—within our mind, for it is through coming to know our mind that we can come to know ourselves. And in coming to know ourselves, we can live a life full of joy and contentment, and be able to benefit others at the same time.

Meditation has been one of the greatest gifts I have been given. I bow down in appreciation to my teachers and the spiritual friends who have taught me. Coming to know my mind has been the most fulfilling and profound path I've taken in my life. I look forward to sharing it with you.

Chapter 1

An Auspicious Beginning

I sometimes ask people, "What is meditation?"

I receive an amazing range of responses. Those who have experience of meditating will often describe an activity that they do, a method, or a technique. They relate a way of concentrating on their breath, or reciting a mantra (a sacred sound, word, or phrase), or visualizing energy and esoteric shapes and colors within their body, or contemplating love or a saint's life. For some people, meditation means simply sitting still for days and weeks on end. Others place their body in yoga postures, or move while controlling their breath. Others will say meditation comes from cutting themselves off from distractions altogether, perhaps by holding their breath for long durations. Others have told me they meditate while running, or preparing tea, or resting their awareness in the gap between wakeful and sleep states.

The vast array of meditation techniques found among spiritual and contemplative traditions can sometimes seem daunting, especially if we want to begin our own meditation practice.

But is meditation just a technique or method? I suggest meditation is *what arises from within us upon applying a method or technique.*

It is often supposed that meditation is a particular mental state—peaceful, relaxed, saintly, or empty. Let's let go of that idea right at the outset. Let's also dispense with the notion that we're trying to stop our thoughts when we meditate, or that we must sit in full lotus position to do so. In fact, it's useful to free ourselves from any such concept or labeling about meditation at all.

Meditation is not a singular, steady experience. Rather, it is a dynamic and continual process, an unfolding of our awareness. Through it, we come to know the entirety of our reality—from sensory stimulation to our thoughts and emotions.

Going deeper, meditation is a familiarity with the working of our mind and our perception that is never static but always flowing. And what flows before our lucid awareness in meditation is the ever-changing reality that we call the present.

I think of meditation as a vehicle, or what supports us on a journey inward. Our journey may traverse the dark valleys and scary ridgelines of our scattered, distracted, and confused being. But as we persevere, we discover our inherent qualities of pristine wisdom, abiding intelligence, and unbound compassion.

For this book, I suggest a working definition for meditation as: *coming to know the mind.*

Why meditate?

There are many reasons for meditating. It seems to me that one of the main ones is to enjoy contentment. When we look at our life, contentment is usually fleeting. Instead, we often live day to day with a sense of lack, of dissatisfaction, of dis-ease.

We all, regardless of nationality, religion, or beliefs, want to experience contentment in our life. We want something beyond feeling happy, because deep down we know that our feelings come and go like the clouds in the sky.

Contentment comes from within—from deep within our being. But the circumstances of our life and the actions of our body, speech and mind often prevent this contentment from rising up to express itself. Instead, we are caught up in looking for contentment in things—in food, in relationships, in money, in situations, and in fleeting experiences that, while they might be temporarily enjoyable, eventually dissolve, and then we are left with that familiar sense of lack.

Meditation can be a skillful means of discovering contentment. It takes us within ourselves, and points us in the direction of where contentment is found. As the Dalai Lama has explained, "Granted, external circumstances can contribute to one's happiness and well-being, but ultimately happiness and suffering depend upon the mind, and how it perceives."

Cultivating the mind

Meditation isn't a religion, and it certainly isn't based upon any dogma. We don't have to be a Buddhist monk, Hindu yogi, or Jewish or Christian mystic to meditate. We can meditate and still maintain our own religious practice. Or no religion at all. I meditate with people of all faiths, as well as those who don't have any spiritual or religious beliefs, and they find great value in their practice. The methods of meditation you will learn in this book can be incorporated into any faith, or practiced in a completely secular manner.

I myself have pursued a predominantly Buddhist approach. In the Buddhist tradition, there are many skillful means of understanding how this mind of ours works. These include contemplation, logical inquiry and philosophical debate, as well as the experiential path of meditation. We will focus on the direct path of the meditator, which relies upon our own clear discernment rather than inference, faith, belief, or intellectual speculation. I will use some Buddhist examples and references in the book.

One of the words that the Buddha is said to have used to describe meditation is *bhavana*, a Pali word, which means "to cultivate." What we are cultivating in meditation is the mind.

For most of us, our mind has been cultivated to inquire into and know about the world around us. We can know the exact temperature outside at any given moment and what time of day tomorrow it is expected to rain. We can look far into the galaxy and listen to what moves in the depths of the ocean. We can communicate almost as fast as the speed of light and have a USB stick containing the scriptures of every religious faith on the planet. Mathematics, biology, physics and other sciences have given us incredible depth of knowledge about our external world.

In meditation, we aren't focusing so much on the external world, but are turning our direction of inquiry within, to work with our mind. We aren't setting out to gain knowledge, but to search for experiential understanding and insight.

I am talking about an inner *bhavana*, an inner science, an inner knowledge—seeing how our mind functions, perceives and knows, and also how it distorts, veils, and distracts.

A meditator's toolbox

Our inner cultivation of the mind, our meditation practice, begins with developing mental tools like single-pointed concentration, mindfulness, spaciousness, and undistracted awareness, to name just a few—we will examine these later on.

Once we have developed these mental tools, we use them to look not only at what the mind perceives—sights, sounds, tastes, scents, touch, and thoughts—but at the mind itself. This is to say that through meditation we can become intimately aware of awareness. Our attention need not be continually hijacked by distractions and taken away into endless thinking and thought loops about the past that doesn't exist and the future that hasn't arisen. Rather, through meditation, our awareness is allowed to manifest fully its lucid and spacious qualities.

It is said that this kind of inner cultivation of the mind leads us to a state of equanimity, balance, and deep mental wellbeing with a sense of ease, even during our hectic lives.

It is further suggested that meditation can lead toward discerning the root causes of our own dissatisfaction and suffering, and, significantly, how we might uproot those causes altogether. This is what the great meditation masters of the past tell us.

But we don't have to take their word for it. We need to test, to experience, to inquire and see if meditation brings us any benefit at all. Even though the Buddha said that meditation was the direct path to uncovering the wisdom within us, still we must test the practices ourselves.

"Just as the wise test the purity of gold by burning, cutting and examining it by means of a piece of touchstone," the Buddha said, "so should you accept my words after examining them and not merely out of regard and reverence for me."

So we'll begin with meditation practices that settle and calm our body and mind. Once we've achieved some stability and can remain undistracted for a period of time, we'll investigate the nature of our experience, our world, and our reality. We'll use a focused, calm, and sharply attentive mind to look deeply into our own experience and come to very clear conclusions about those experiences.

Meditation practice is best applied progressively, day after day, with diligence, and a healthy dose of humor and joy. For the meditation practices in this book, I encourage you to spend a week or two, or more, with each chapter. Develop some proficiency with the various techniques before moving on. Repetition is one of the keys to the practice. There's no need to rush.

Instead, become well accustomed to using different mental tools—like mindfulness, concentration, acceptance, spaciousness, and inquiry—to train your mind and deepen your meditation practice. These tools will help you hone your emotional agility, cultivate mental balance, and discern reality as it is. Knowing when and how to cultivate various aspects of the mind is a great skill—on and off the meditation cushion.

I trust that the meditative tools in this book will point you in a direction where you can come to know yourself in the deepest and innermost way. The techniques are straightforward, and the results can be profound. In seeing clearly and viscerally how our mind works, we find insights into the true source of contentedness arising quite naturally. These insights, which occur in meditation sessions and in the post-meditation period throughout the day, have far-reaching consequences, because we gain an inner strength that is based in the reality of our present experience. And liberation is found in the continual awareness of the reality of the present moment, right here, right now.

This is what I am keen to offer to you—the great freedom that results from coming to know one's own mind. When we truly know our own mind, we can begin to work skillfully with all of the challenges in our life in a more real and grounded manner.

Where to begin?

I am sometimes asked, "What do I need to begin a meditation practice?"

The most important thing is an open and inquisitive attitude. This type of attitude is imbued with enthusiasm. Enthusiasm will be needed, because the path of the meditator is not always smooth, or calm, or relaxing.

It is important to recognize this from the beginning. We are seeking to know our mind and discern reality clearly, not to have particular kinds of blissful or happy experiences. When we meditate, we might feel blissful or happy, but we'll also likely feel tired or frustrated. We'll work with *all* of our experiences within the context of meditation and they will help us come to know our mind ever more deeply. We aren't meditating to escape from the complexities and stress of life, but rather to be, as the poet T.S. Eliot described, a still point as the world turns around us.

Thinking back to my first years of meditation practice, there are several things I wish I'd known then. I suspect my teacher told me these things, but I didn't hear them!

Top things I wish I'd known at the start

- ❖ Meditation isn't about having a special kind of feeling.
- ❖ Meditation isn't always chilled, blissful, or relaxing.
- ❖ Meditation isn't about stopping thoughts.

◆ Meditation doesn't just occur on a cushion, but can happen anywhere, anytime.

◆ Meditation isn't retreating from the world, but engaging more deeply with it.

◆ Meditation isn't a singular, steady experience that we try to return to, but an ever-changing process.

◆ Meditation isn't about trying to be spiritual. It's about seeing reality as it is.

Please keep these points in mind.

I suggest you keep a journal about your meditation practice. You can use it as minimally as noting down the type of your daily meditation and the length of time you practiced, but if you'd like to write more extensively about your feelings about the practice, that would be great. I especially encourage you to write down any insights that you have during your meditation, or in the post-meditation period.

I once asked a teenager with whom I was meditating if she had any particular insights during her meditation practice and she said, "I realized that I don't have to have an opinion about every thought that shoots through my head."

I smiled and said, "Write that down in your journal and remember that!"

As well as a journal, you'll need a place to sit, or lie down, comfortably still for your meditation practice. Ideally, this is a quiet place where you can remain undisturbed and leave your phone and other electronics in another room. We'll talk about different postures later on, but wherever you can sit with straight back will suffice.

While it is beneficial to have a dedicated meditation space, perhaps with a beautiful shrine, special meditation cushions upon which to assume full lotus position, fine Japanese incense and other accoutrements, meditation is really about coming to know our mind—the rest is lovely decoration!

Something else to bring to your meditation practice is a clear motivation. Why do you want to meditate? What is it that you want from your meditation practice?

We all meditate for different reasons. Some of us use meditation to be calm or to quieten our mind before we start a day that will be full of stressful situations. Others need meditation to deal with a habit of being frustrated or angry. Some people might have an expansive vision of meditating to become closer to the sacred and divine, while others see it as a direct path to awakening and enlightenment. Whatever the reason, it's good for us to be very clear with ourselves about why we are choosing to meditate.

"Good in the beginning"

In the Buddhist and Hatha Yoga traditions, meditation was usually taught only after the student had firmly established a moral and ethical framework. Why was this?

Some of the mental skills that are developed in meditation, like mindfulness and concentration, aren't in themselves positive or negative—they're just skills. And they can be used for benefit or harm. A skilled sniper almost certainly has superior concentration skills, though they are used to kill. A corporate executive might meditate to have a steady, cool mind so they can swindle others in shady business deals. Robbing a bank most certainly will be better accomplished if the bandit is utterly mindful at every step.

So we use a moral compass to ensure that our meditation practice isn't used to increase our anger, greed, or non-virtuous behavior. In the Buddhist tradition in which I was trained, there is a saying, "Good in the beginning, good in the middle, and good in the end." When we apply this to our meditation practice, "good in the beginning" means that we remind ourselves that we aren't only meditating for ourselves, but to benefit others as well. At least we can have that aspiration.

How can our meditation practice benefit others? A friend of mine who'd been meditating with me for six months had never really believed that her practice could benefit others. She told me she'd been content with the joy and peace that her practice had brought her. But that changed one day unexpectedly.

After we'd meditated together one afternoon, she took the bus home. The bus encountered a traffic jam and many upset travelers began yelling at the bus driver, cursing the snail-pace traffic, and generally being loud. My friend took the opportunity to continue meditating on the bus, observing her in-breath and out-breath as the raucous bus ride continued.

After more than an hour, during which all the other passengers left angrily, she reached her stop at the end of the line. As she departed, the driver told her, "I really noticed your calm presence. Thank you. With all those people yelling, I don't know what I'd have done without that comfort."

Our meditation practice reverberates beyond us, even when we aren't aware of it. So, before each of our meditation sessions, we establish our motivation and express our goodwill by thinking something like:

> *May my practice of meditation bring clarity of the mind and softness of the heart so that I may be more loving and compassionate in my family, in my community, and beyond.*

We are, in effect, extending the sphere of benefit from ourselves to others. So that is "good in the beginning."

"Good in the middle" means that whatever meditation practice we do, we do it with an attitude that is fresh and open, free of grasping hopes or tentative fear. We don't worry if we are meditating "correctly" or "getting it right." We just practice.

Then, at the conclusion of our meditation session, we gather our mind, our heart and our intention together and mentally share whatever virtue or positivity has come from our practice. Whom do we share it with? With everyone we brought to mind in our original motivation—those in our family, our community, and beyond—meaning everyone! This is "good in the end." It is known as "dedication."

Practice: Motivation and dedication

Take a moment to consider your motivation for meditating and then jot it down in your journal, perhaps in a short verse form suitable for contemplation at the beginning of your formal meditation session.

For "good in the beginning" you might consider:

Through this session of meditation,

May I develop clarity of mind and softness of heart,

So that I can more skillfully benefit

Those in my family, in my community, and beyond.

And for your dedication, "good in the end," you might have something like:

> *Through the power and virtue of my meditation practice today,*
>
> *May the benefit not only remain with me,*
>
> *But may it ripple into the world,*
>
> *Bringing deep contentment and alleviating suffering for others.*

These may change over time, and that's fine, but it's always good to start and seal our practice in an auspicious way.

Chapter 2

Cultivating Stillness
and Comfort

The two most important aspects for settling into a formal meditation practice are stillness and comfort. A motionless body is a conducive container for meditation, but allowing the body to be absolutely still can be a challenge for many of us. And it isn't always comfortable.

Still, if we arrange our body in the most comfortable position for us, either seated or lying down, once we find that position, we can just let our body be without fussing or adjusting. And, with a little effort and perseverance, we can find comfort and ease in our posture. I'll discuss a little later different stretching and yoga postures that help us find this comfortable meditation posture.

We cultivate stillness of the body in meditation because when we move the body, it tends to stir up thoughts and thinking, which may lead to a distracted mind. We're not trying to block thoughts while learning to meditate but we are trying to minimize distraction.

We'll have all kinds of experiences, mental and physical, in meditation, and pain will sometimes arise in our body. While we're not looking to have discomfort or pain when we meditate, oftentimes it provides the context for us to learn about our reactions and ourselves. This too I'll discuss in more detail a bit later.

Connecting body and mind through body scanning

One of the most common meditation techniques in the Buddhist tradition is known as body scanning. It was the very first method to which I was introduced.

Body scanning gathers our attention, which is so often scattered outwardly, chasing after sights, sounds, and thoughts, and redirects it. We collect our attention, bring our mind into our body and scan our body to feel the physical, tactile sensations that are happening right here, right now. This tends to release the body from tension and the mind from stress, and for this reason it is often a preliminary meditation practice. But body scanning can also be a complete practice by itself, and I know nuns and monks in Burma and Thailand who use it as their principal meditation practice for their entire lives.

The method, or technique, is quite simple. We place our attention for a few moments on different locations on our body—each about the size of a baby's handprint—and feel whatever tactile sensations are present—tingling, numbness, warmth, coolness, itching, hardness, or softness. Then we move our attention to another location, continuing like this in a set pattern over the entire body.

We observe the sensations in a raw and direct manner. We aren't thinking about them, or questioning what we're feeling. We don't have to name or label them. We're simply witnessing, or observing, sensation in a very open and relaxed manner.

At the same time as we're observing the tactile sensations, we're also noticing how they change, shift, move, arise and dissipate. And, as we're observing them, we may notice an accompanying sense of like or dislike. Some sensations may be pleasant. Others may not be so pleasant. Some sensations may be more neutral.

Whatever the case, we simply observe each tactile sensation, and if there is an accompanying pleasant, unpleasant, or neutral feeling, we observe that too. There's no need to push away a sensation or try to change it. We don't have to ask ourselves, "Is this pleasant or not?" We just observe in a very relaxed and attentive way.

Sensations change moment to moment, hour to hour, day to day. Perhaps we feel our foot throbbing one moment and then it transitions into a soothing feeling.

Even the throbbing feeling itself is an example of change. Can we watch this process of change happen?

We might notice how the sensations of our body often spur our mind into thought loops, where we no longer experience what is actually happening in the present, but go off on long mental narratives. These narratives are often fueled by our attachments and aversions, and most often have little correlation with reality. When we notice that our mind has moved away from the awareness of tactile sensations, we release the thinking, relax, and come back to the meditation practice.

When we focus our attention on the sensations of our body, we very quickly begin to see how we become bored, or excited, or sleepy, or anxious, or a whole host of other types of emotion or moods. When we notice this, again we just relax and return to scanning the body.

Body-scanning meditation connects us to the unfolding process of change. This is not an intellectual affair, but a visceral knowing. We avail ourselves of new insights into the changing nature of our world, right here in our own body.

As we practice, we may find that we can experience pleasant sensations without clinging to them. And that we can experience unpleasant ones, even pain, without fear.

As we progress in the practice of body scanning, we can find freedom in whatever arises and dissolves. We see it, connect with it, and know it. And a deep learning happens along with it.

I first practiced body-scanning meditation in Nepal. I entered a 10-day Vipassana retreat with a group of 30 other meditators on a hillside above Kathmandu. We meditated for 10 sessions each day, and each session lasted 45–75 minutes. We took silent walking breaks in between the sessions. The first meditation session started well before sunrise and our last session was at 8:30 at night. It was an austere setting and we did not speak, read books or even write in our journals for the entire 10 days. And our last meal was at 12 noon! Hour after hour, each day, we sat on the floor and scanned our body.

Of course I had some pain in my body and struggles in my mind with my resistance and emotions—we all do. But I continued to scan and scan, and scan some more. This might seem a bit extreme as a beginner! Remarkably, the experience was not tedious or boring, but deeply insightful.

There was nothing special about the method, but the results were profound. Looking back, these were perhaps the most important 10 days of my life, because they were a window through which I saw the potential for a contentment that wasn't dependent upon anything at all besides the mind!

On the second day, I felt pain in my lower back. As soon as it came, I was annoyed and began thinking that my whole retreat would be ruined by my inability to sit comfortably. I thought my body "should be strong" and "should not be this way." I started thinking about the different yoga postures that I'd need to do after the retreat to strengthen my back. And my mind shot backward, wondering exactly when it was that I'd twisted my back. Perhaps my rucksack had been too heavy when I'd been trekking near Mount Everest, or maybe it had happened when I'd been injured during middle school football, or maybe I'd even crawled in a weird way when I was an infant.

I battled my mind with future thinking and thinking about the past, especially when I scanned my lower back and came to that sensation. It was as if that sensation was not only the most important thing in the world, but something that would never, ever, go away.

I continued the meditation retreat, and by the fourth or fifth day, as I continually returned to that sensation during the scanning process, I noticed that it was hot in the middle and the heat dissipated into a kind of cool ring around the edge. I saw that a subtle throbbing was stronger in the morning than in the evening. And I don't know exactly when, but eventually the label of "pain" seemed to fade away, and by the middle of the week, my association of pain with that sensation had completely disappeared. By Day 10, that place on my lower back was one of the places in my body where I observed sensation, change, and my habitual reactions. That was all. And it was profound.

I'm not encouraging anyone to try to cultivate painful experiences. But this example showed me how a sensation that I once called "pain" became a real teacher for me, pointing me toward knowing my mind and habits in a deeper way.

I'll take you through a guided body-scanning meditation in a moment, but first a word about meditation posture.

Alertness in our meditation posture

In any meditation posture—seated, standing, walking, or lying down—it's important to maintain an alert position. Alertness is facilitated by a straight but not rigid spine. Your head is balanced between your shoulders. Slightly tuck your chin under in a gesture of introspection. Pull your shoulders back and then relax them. Slightly lift your sternum. Your hands can rest comfortably in your lap or on your knees if you are seated.

The eyes are very important in meditation. People new to meditation are often instructed to close their eyes, because visual stimuli can distract us from concentration. I recommend meditating with your eyes relaxed and open, with a downward gaze, looking into the space in front of you but not focusing on a particular place. Keeping your eyes open very much contributes to an alert mind—it is, after all, difficult to fall asleep with your eyes open!

You may want to begin your meditation session with your eyes closed and then open them after a few minutes. I find this particularly helpful in calming my mind at the beginning of a session.

Whether your eyes are open or closed, try to let them be still, not darting or following visual stimulation. Blinking is normal.

Your lips can be slightly open, if that is comfortable. Release any gripping in your jaw. Also relax the back of your tongue and place the tip near your upper palate. The benefits of resting the tongue in this position are that it relaxes the back of the throat and saliva naturally descends without the need to swallow.

Also, try smiling slightly, as this usually relaxes the face.

Sitting

Sitting in a chair or on a bench is a perfectly acceptable meditation position. If you use a chair, or are seated on the floor, I don't recommend reclining against a wall or the back of the chair. However, if your body needs this support to sit comfortably still, by all means lean back. Soft chairs or couches are not recommended, however, because you will tend to slouch after a few minutes.

If you are seated on the ground cross-legged, please note that the elevation of your knees should be below your hips. If your knees don't rest below your hip line, or don't touch the floor, then place a blanket or soft yoga block on the ground so that they rest upon something rather than hovering. In this manner, you cultivate an immovable stillness throughout your entire body, which is ideal for meditation practice.

Seated meditation posture

Cross-legged meditation posture

Seven-point posture for meditation

1. *Legs* crossed if seated on the floor or, if seated in a chair, have your feet flat on the floor. In both cases, your hips should be slightly above your knees.

2. *Hands* resting in your lap or on your knees.

3. *Back* comfortably straight, with the sternum slightly lifted.

4. *Shoulders* pulled slightly back, and relaxed.

5. *Head* comfortably balanced between your shoulders with your chin slightly tucked under.

6. *Mouth* relaxed, with slightly parted lips, and the tip of your tongue lightly touching (or pointing toward) your upper palate.

7. *Eyes* motionless, gazing past the tip of your nose, or softly closed.

Supine

Another posture for meditation is the supine, or lying down, position. Here we're offering support for the body if it is tired, stressed, or in pain. We're talking about a posture that supports the body in deep relaxation, even while we maintain a meditative alertness.

Any of the seated meditation practices that we'll cover in this book can be used with a lying down posture. Do note, however, that if you're already feeling drowsy or groggy, lying down to meditate can be a quick way to fall asleep!

If you are sleepy, it's perhaps best to have a nice cup of tea and then meditate in a seated posture, or do a walking meditation (*see page 99*), which tends to energize our attention. Remember, in meditation we're coming to know the mind, and to do so, we cultivate both relaxation and attentiveness.

As for the supine posture, it can be as easy as simply extending your body while prone on your back. Some of you may be familiar with *shavasana*, or the corpse posture in yoga, and that is a suitable arrangement of the body. But let me give you what I feel is the most conducive supine posture for meditation.

- Take a seated position and arrange a blanket or bolster under the back of your knees. As you lie back, this provides a bit of support under your slightly bent legs. If you wish, you can place a folded blanket under your shoulders, because this can help relax the shoulders and neck and open the chest.

- It is good to place a pillow, soft yoga block or some other support under the back of your head. This is not only comfy, but it moves the chin down in that gesture of introspection that tends to lead the mind away from distractions.

- If you wish, you can place pillows under your arms as they rest at a 30-degree angle from the body. Your hands can be turned slightly upward.

- If it's cool in the room, it's nice to place a blanket over your body. (Know that if you get too warm, it may cause a bit of drowsiness.)

Supine posture

Finally, one note of caution: when you finish your meditation lying down, be very careful about the manner in which you sit up. Your body may be very relaxed and you don't want to aggravate any back, shoulder or neck muscles with sudden movement. Please get in the habit of:

- bending your knees with your feet flat on the floor; pausing

- then rolling over to one side; pausing again,

- and then slowly pushing yourself up with your arms.

Please don't thrust yourself up, as in a sit-up, from the supine or rolled-over position. Be gentle and careful with your back and body.

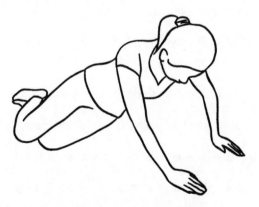

Exiting from the supine posture

Guided meditation: Body scanning

Here is a guided body-scanning meditation for you. It is a complete practice and I recommend you acquaint yourself with it through repeated sessions of 10 minutes each. Within a session, you might scan your body two or three times.

Assume a comfortable seated posture in a chair or on a cushion on the floor, where you can remain still for about 10 minutes. If it's painful to sit still for 10 minutes, you can lie down in a comfortable position.

In either case, try to have your spine straight and your body motionless during the practice.

Formal meditation practice begins with settling your body, speech, and mind in their natural states of equilibrium.

Rest your body in comfort and ease—as still as a mountain.

Let your breath ebb and flow naturally like a placid ocean.

And let your mind be as open and spacious as the sky.

Briefly set your motivation for meditating, perhaps by thinking:

> *Through this session of meditation, may I benefit from clarity of mind and softness of heart, so that I may take those benefits and share them with my family, with my community, and beyond.*

Then gather your mind and feel the tactile sensation of your whole body remaining motionless.

If you wish, take a few deep breaths—full inhalations and relaxing exhalations. And then return to natural breathing.

Allow your spine to be comfortably straight. Let your eyes be open and softly gazing downward. Or, if you wish, gently close your eyes. Whether your eyes are open or closed, allow them to remain as motionless as possible. Blinking is normal.

You have placed your body on the cushion; now bring your mind into your body. Join your body and mind.

Then bring your awareness to whatever part of your body is touching the floor—feel the sides or soles of your feet.

Notice the feeling on the sides or soles of your feet. Concentrate lightly and notice whatever tactile sensations are there—vibrating, pulsating, numbness, perhaps a coolness or warmth.

If you don't feel any sensations as you scan that part of your body, that's no problem. Just feel the lack of sensation.

Then move your awareness to the sides or back and sides of your knees. Again, feel the tactile sensations. You may notice how they change as you observe them. Just observe. There's no need to think about what you are observing.

If your mind begins to think about something else—if it moves away on a thought loop—when you notice this, release the thinking, relax, and return to the practice. No problem.

Then feel the back of your thighs for a few moments. Then your sit-bones pushing into the chair or the floor. Maybe feel the downward gravitational pull at your seat.

If the sensation is pleasant, just feel that. If it is unpleasant, just feel that. If it is neutral, just feel that. There's no need to react, change or alter anything. Simply relax and remain present with the felt experience.

Then move your awareness to the base of your spine. Again, simply feel the sensations. There's no need to think about them. Just feel them. Pleasant—let it be. Unpleasant—let it be. Neutral—let it be.

Slowly move your awareness from your tail bone up your spine to your mid-back, between your shoulders, and the back of your neck. There's no need to adjust anything. Simply feel.

Then spread your awareness over the back of your head and behind your ears, finally arriving at the crown of your head. Remain there momentarily to feel the sensation at the fontanel.

Next, continuing to keep your body very still, move your attention over your forehead, temples, and eyebrows, and feel the sensations there. If there is tension, you can release it.

Feel your eyes and all the muscles around your eyes.

Then your cheeks, jaws, and the back of your tongue.

Next, bring your attention to your nostrils, perhaps feeling the warm or cool air passing in and out of your nose. Just feel.

And then move your attention to your lips. What sensations do you notice?

Your attention continues to descend over your chin and pauses over your chest. Perhaps you feel the slight beat of your heart. Or your skin against the fabric of your shirt or blouse.

Finally, let your awareness descend into your belly region, which you can allow to be loose and relaxed. There's no need to hold the belly in with tension. Feel the tactile sensation of the movement of your belly, in and out, as you breathe naturally.

If you wish, return to the soles of your feet and scan your body again.

Finally, continuing to keep your body motionless, relax the mental effort you have exerted to notice the tactile sensations in your body. Rest for a few moments in silent stillness.

Conclude with a brief dedication:

> *Through the power and virtue of my meditation practice today, may any benefit not only remain with me, but ripple into the world to bring deep contentment and alleviate suffering for others.*

Now I encourage you to write about your experience in your meditation journal.

The breath, our companion on the path of meditation

The Buddha recommended concentrating on many different objects to support our meditation practice. Some were physical, such as bodily sensations, or visual, such as a pool of water or pinholes with the light shining through. Some were mental, such as our thoughts, emotions and mental images. There were sounds, tastes and even scents too that he suggested as supports for our concentration. A number of these practices will be included in this book. But the object, or support, for meditation practice that the Buddha suggested most often was the breath.

There are a variety of reasons why concentrating on the breath, or more specifically, the repeating pattern of inhalation and exhalation and the slight pauses in between, is particularly useful:

- First, focusing on the breath has a calming effect on the body and mind and facilitates single-pointed concentration.

- Secondly, whether we are aware of our breath or not, it continues reflexively. So it is very dependable because it is always there for us.

- Thirdly, concentrating on the breath generally doesn't arouse strong emotions that can spur us into distracted thinking. One of my teachers used to say, "If I give you a golden Buddha statue to concentrate on, after a short while you might start thinking, 'Why did he give me such a small statue?' or 'I like the way the eyes are painted on that other statue,' and so on."

When we use the breath as a support in our meditation practice, we needn't alter or change how we are breathing, as we may when we are doing yoga postures or yogic breathing. Here, we aren't trying to breathe deeper, longer or in any particular manner; we're simply observing the way the breath presents itself. We're placing our attention upon it very lightly, like a butterfly landing upon a flower, and riding the physical sensation of the entire cycle of in-breath, out-breath, and slight pauses in between.

We place our attention wherever we feel the breath most prominently, which is likely to be either around the nostril region, the chest, or the belly. As we breathe in, we may feel cool air passing through our nostrils and into our sinus passages or lungs. We might feel the rise and fall of our chest or belly, or our skin slightly moving against our clothing. As we exhale, we may feel warm air moving out of our nostrils, and our body slightly sinking.

There may other physical sensations within our body as we watch our breath. Perhaps we notice a more energized feeling on the inhalation and a settling, relaxed sensation when we breathe out.

As we watch the ebb and flow of our breath, we may notice its texture too. Maybe it's long and smooth. Or perhaps rough and halting.

Every breath is new, different than before, and an opportunity to continually refresh our attention.

Guided meditation: Discovering the breath

Arrange your body in a comfortable and stable meditation posture, either seated or lying down. Create a steady foundation with your legs and hips and feet, and once you find it, let them remain there, steady like a mountain.

Arising from your foundation is your comfortably straight spine. Pull your shoulders slightly back and then relax them. Balance your head between your shoulders and tuck your chin under slightly.

Your lips can be slightly parted and your tongue gently placed at the front of your upper palate. Your eyes can be gently closed or partially open—in either case, relax them and keep them from darting here and there.

Now, having adjusted your posture, you can adjust your attitude, perhaps by thinking,

> *May the benefit accrued today through my efforts in meditation not only remain with me but be shared with my family, my community, and beyond.*

To begin, take a few deep breaths—full inhalations and complete exhalations—then let your breath return to its natural rhythm.

Bring your awareness to your body for a short while. Feel your body as a composite whole as you relax into stillness.

Next, gather your mind and bring it into your body. Feel the physical sensations of sitting still for a few moments.

Then, move your awareness to whatever part of you is touching the floor. Feel the tactile sensations of the bottom or sides of your feet, your shins, the back of your thighs and your sit-bones.

Next, move your awareness to the base of your spine and slowly scan up your back, feeling the tactile sensations as your awareness passes over your sacrum, lower and mid-back, and between your shoulders.

Move up to the head, spreading your awareness over your scalp and behind your ears, until you arrive at the crown of your head. Just feel whatever tactile sensations are present.

Then scan slowly down the front of your body. Feel your forehead, temples, and eyes. Release any tension. Let your face be heavy. Relax your jaw and the back of your tongue.

Continue scanning down, over your lips and chin to your chest, perhaps feeling the beat of your heart.

Finally, arrive in your belly region, which you can allow to be loose and relaxed.

Now, as you continue keeping your body very still, move your attention to your nostril and lip region. Locate the feeling of your breath in the area.

Lightly place your attention upon your breath, and begin to follow the movement and feeling of the inhalation, exhalation, and the slight pauses in between.

Remain very relaxed, and very attentive of your breath around your nostril and lip region.

If you recognize you're thinking about something else, just release the thinking, relax, and return to the practice. However many times you are distracted, release, relax and return to the practice. Return to the breath.

Watch the natural flow of the breath, observing the movement, the feeling, and the texture. Breathing in... Breathing out... There's no need to prefer one kind of breath over the other. Simply watch the breath.

Meditate in this manner for five or 10 minutes.

Then, keeping your body very still, let go of concentrating on your breath, and rest in silent stillness for a few moments.

To conclude with a dedication, perhaps you may think:

> *With whatever benefit comes from my meditation practice, may I breathe joy and love into the world.*

What to do with all of these thoughts?

When I started meditating, my practice for the first two years was body scanning and breath meditation. I remember feeling in the first week that I was having many more thoughts and was much more distracted than ever before. I asked my monk teacher, "Is this meditating upon my body and breath making me more distracted?"

He smiled and said, "No, you just never noticed your distracted mind before. Your distracted mind was normal. Now that is changing."

When we begin to meditate, it may seem that we've never been so distracted. We may notice that this mind of ours thinks about anything and everything. When we try to concentrate for a few moments, our mind seems to rebel and want to rehash long-gone memories or endlessly plan the future. One thought triggers another, and within minutes, a chain reaction of thoughts ricochets through our mind. Thinking can move at an incredibly fast pace. The irony is that often we aren't even aware of what we're thinking about!

As my teacher pointed out to me, before I started meditating I'd never taken the time to notice how I mindlessly engaged in endless thought loops throughout the day. Initially it seemed as though I didn't have a choice in the matter—my thoughts required me to think about them. But very quickly, through meditation, I realized that I did have a choice.

Having thoughts and thinking about those thoughts during meditation are absolutely normal. In fact, as one of my Tibetan teachers told me, "If you never have thoughts, you are probably a corpse!" But while we might not have fewer thoughts in meditation, our relationship to our thoughts changes. We realize that we don't have to think about every thought.

In meditation, thoughts need not leave any more imprints on the mind than a hawk's soaring leaves an impression on the sky.

Mindfulness

To gain some control over our wildly distractible mind, we rein it in with the rope of mindfulness.

Mindfulness is, to use the definition given by an accomplished fourth-century CE meditator by the name of Asanga in his book *The Compendium of Higher Teachings* (*Abhidharmasamuccaya*), "the non-forgetfulness of the mind with regard to a familiar object. Its function is non-distraction."

The word "mindfulness" is a translation of a Pali term, *sati*, which means "to return" or "to recall." We use mindfulness to bring ourselves back to whatever we have chosen to concentrate upon, such as physical sensations, the breath, or thoughts and emotions. Just as Asanga indicated, we are returning to and recalling our object of concentration.

Mindfulness is, therefore, the antidote to distraction, and is an essential mental tool for the meditator. When we continually apply it in our practice, the result is a pliable and agile mind.

It is said in the Buddhist scriptures that when we first apply mindfulness, much effort is needed, and this is called *deliberate mindfulness*. After some steadiness has been attained and mindfulness can be applied without too much mental exertion, it is called *effortless mindfulness*. Once it is a way of being rather than a practice, it is what the Buddha called *genuine mindfulness*. And a mind that is simply never distracted has *King-like mindfulness*.

You might consider how mindfulness is useful in daily life and write about it in your meditation journal.

Release, relax, and return

An essential part of our meditation practice is to notice when we are distracted. Sometimes we notice right away when we start thinking or are distracted by a sound or something else around us, or a rising emotion. Other times we might not even realize how long we've been away on a thought loop. The important point is noticing when we've moved away from the object of our concentration.

What do we do when we notice we are distracted? What do we do when we catch ourselves thinking? We simply release the thinking, relax, and return to the chosen object.

Release, relax, and return to the practice—it seems so simple. Yet again and again we run up against our own entrenched habit of chasing our thoughts. So, each time we notice, we have to do it again: release, relax, and return to the practice. Like any mental skill, it takes practice.

When we notice we are distracted, there's no need to think about *why* we were thinking, because this is, of course, another layer of thinking, which is not our intention at this time. We don't have to do anything except release the thinking, relax, and return.

Some traditions instruct us to note mentally, *Thought*, or *Thinking*, and then come back to the practice. I do not recommend that here. Instead, we use the awareness of our distracted mind to return mindfully to the practice.

The consequence of returning our attention to our object of concentration is that worries, fears, and stress are released. Each time we notice our distractions, we are given an opportunity to relax!

There is also a subtle but important point that I want to highlight: we are not trying to block thoughts. Rather, we are releasing ourselves from thinking. If we try to block and suppress thoughts, we will become frustrated very quickly. So, instead, we release the thinking.

When we release and relax, a thought may seem to linger, but we are not thinking about it. It is not unlike when a child releases a helium-filled balloon—it remains for a time, but gradually drifts away.

Release, relax, and return to your practice with joy.

Being kind to ourselves

A common mental habit or pattern in people new to meditation is being overly critical of themselves and how distracted they are. I know this trait very well, because for the first couple of years I meditated, I had a running commentary inside my head about my practice. The commentary occurred on and off the meditation cushion.

The voice inside my head scolded me for the kinds of thoughts I had, and that I was having thoughts at all as I sat in full lotus. "After all," the voice reminded me, "I'm meditating in the high Himalayas with venerable Tibetan Buddhist masters! I should be like all the yogis I've been reading about who speedily purified their minds and gained enlightenment!"

I was very hard on myself, which resulted in pushing too hard in my meditation sessions, and this led to physical and mental maladies.

When my monk teacher recognized what was happening, he offered two gems of advice, which I still regularly recall. I find nearly all of us can benefit from this advice at different points on our journey of meditation.

First, he told me to remember that our awareness is like the sky, spacious and very clear, and our thoughts and emotions are like the clouds. Some clouds are delicate and thin and travel quickly, and other clouds are darker and ominously fill the sky. But no matter what kind of clouds appear, the spaciousness and clarity of the sky remain. They may be temporarily obscured, but they are always there.

"Rest in the spaciousness and clarity of your awareness. And have patience," he told me.

Secondly, he counseled, "Be kind to yourself."

Noticing when we are distracted in meditation (or in daily life) is not only a moment to release the thinking and relax, it is also a time when we can let go of the inner voice that tells us that we have failed for being distracted, or criticizes us in some other way.

Becoming aware of our distracted, confused and muddled mind is actually a golden moment, because we can immediately practice kindness toward ourselves.

"With gentleness and spaciousness, release the thinking, relax, and return to your practice," my teacher told me.

Eight tips for establishing a daily meditation practice

Now you know a little more about meditation and have had a taste of body scanning and meditating on the breath, here are some tips for establishing a daily meditation practice.

1. Remind yourself of your motivation

Look back at the motivation for meditating that you wrote down in your journal. Remind yourself of it before each meditation session. Perhaps write a new motivation from time to time.

2. Short sessions, many times

Keep the length of your meditation sessions on the shorter side, especially at the beginning. I suggest meditating daily for 10–20 minutes.

The point is to practice with relaxed alertness. It is more beneficial to have a short session of alert attentiveness than it is to sit sleepily for 45 minutes. Try to conclude your session when you are still fresh and wouldn't mind continuing. Slowly increase the length and frequency of formal sessions, but not past the point of freshness.

As for how to keep track of how long you meditate, I recommend having a clock in the room that is not on your smartphone (leave your phone outside your meditation space). You can also find sand-timers easily—these are a wonderful option.

3. Keep your practice close to your heart

My first Tibetan Buddhist meditation teacher told me, "Don't tell anyone you meditate." I didn't understand immediately what he meant, but today I do. In the beginning, sometimes our enthusiasm can take over and we can talk a lot about meditation but meditate very little. Consider redirecting that enthusiastic energy inward to fuel your meditation practice.

That said, it's good to let your partners or close friends know what you're doing so they can lend support as you establish a daily meditation practice.

4. Establish a routine

We form habits very quickly—both positive and negative habits. We can use this tendency to our advantage in our daily meditation practice by establishing a routine.

Perhaps you sit and meditate immediately after your coffee or tea is made. Or right after your yoga practice—each time. One of my friends waits in her church pew at the end of the service and meditates.

Perhaps your days are so full that you need to schedule your meditation time in your daily planner—if so, schedule it. Initially it will take some effort and discipline, but soon your interest will increase and you will establish the habit.

Strive on, with ease, because, as the Buddha said in the *Fundamentals of the Path* (*Dhammapada*), "A disciplined mind brings happiness."

5. Commit

Make a commitment to a formal meditation session each day for a certain period. You can write it down in your journal, for example: "I will meditate for 10 minutes every day for the next month."

Go easy on yourself, though—remember, short sessions, many times. It is better to meditate for 10 minutes every day for a month than for one hour on a random weekend.

One of my teachers says that establishing a daily meditation practice "is like brushing your teeth—we do it a few times each day, rather than waiting until Sunday and brushing for an hour. If you do that, it will be painful, not very useful, and probably you'll see some blood! Every day you brush—every day you meditate."

6. Practice when you practice

When you sit down to meditate, just meditate. There's no need to check your email on your smartphone one last time. Or to stretch your body extensively. When it's time to practice, just practice. Body still. Speech silent. Mind spacious and alert. No need to waste time arranging this and that.

Also, know what method you're going to practice and just practice that method. You may have many methods in your meditation toolbox, but use one for each session, and maybe stick with that for a week, or a month, or longer.

Like an infant grabbing one colorful toy and then tossing it to grab another, the mind sometimes wants to switch between meditation methods during the session. But it's better for it to become agile at one method through repeated practice than to move between many.

7. Keep a book of insights

Note down in your journal any insights that arise during your formal meditation session, or perhaps afterwards as you go about your day. Every so often, re-read your insights as a reminder to yourself.

8. Rejoice

At the conclusion of your daily meditation practice, before jumping off your cushion and rushing into your day, savor the moment. In this solitary time, rejoice and give thanks for the fortunate circumstances that allow you to cultivate a path of introspection and meditation. Remember that you are blessed to have this opportunity.

Rejoicing in our own, and others' good fortune is a way of energizing our practice. Even after meditation sessions that we have found frustrating, boring, or even painful, we can be glad that we have made a sustained effort to cultivate clarity of mind and softness of heart.

Chapter 3

Discerning Reality

As our meditation practice develops, once our body is calm and able to remain motionless, our thoughts and emotions tend to slow down slightly. Then we apply a method of concentration, like observing bodily sensations or our breath, and use the rope of mindfulness to bring ourselves back when we become distracted.

We also cultivate a spaciously relaxed disposition while meditating. And as we develop single-pointed concentration, a non-distracted state of being arises.

After honing our ability to remain non-distracted, we are then able to direct our attention to our present experience with a panoramic awareness.

During this process, we are coming to know our mind, and may have glimpses of reality as it is—beyond our thoughts and emotions and interpretations. But often it is just a glimpse. What will allow those glimpses of reality to become more sustained?

Focusing on the present moment

Instead of seeing reality as it is, we are often ruminating about past experiences or embroiled in thinking about the future. Both of these habits obscure seeing reality. The past no longer exists and the future has not arisen. Our task in meditation is to awaken fully to the ever-changing flow that we call the present moment.

As the Buddha said in the Auspicious Day Discourse (Bhaddekaratta Sutta):

No need to chase after the past
or place expectations on the future.
What is past
is left behind.
The future
has not arisen.
Look deeply at life as it is.
In the very here and now,
the meditator develops the heart dwelling in stability
and freedom.
Death can come at any time.
This cannot be disputed.
A practitioner who dwells thus mindfully aware,
throughout the day and night, knows the most
auspicious way to live.

In dwelling mindfully aware in the present moment, we reclaim the power that fear and hope have taken away from us.

It is important to remember that meditation is not a singular occurrence. It is not something we "get" once and then return to. There is no "it" to "get" in meditation practice. What is to be found in meditation is a continual renewal of our awareness in the present moment, which is never the same and always changing. Coming to know our mind is an eternally unfolding process, a peeling away, like pulling back the layers of an onion, one after another, moment by moment, day by day.

Feelings, experiences, emotions, and the like come and go while we are meditating. Many of the insights we have during meditation arise simply through watching the fleeting arising and dissolution of our ephemeral ideas, thoughts, and emotions. Even when we have profound experiences in meditation, such as bodily bliss, vivid clarity, or states of no-thought, they too are impermanent, so we are not trying to return to them. Rather, we are returning to a given method of meditation, through which fresh insights will continually arise from within us.

Strive on! Relax, relax, alert, alert!

Guided meditation: The breath as our companion

Find a comfortable seated meditation posture. Or, if you have some kind of pain or need support, arrange yourself in a supine position.

However you situate yourself, work to bring a steadiness and fresh alertness into your posture with a spine that is straight but not stiff, and eyes that are softly shut or gazing downward without moving.

Relaxing your body, take a few deep breaths—full inhalations, relaxing exhalations. Then return to natural breathing.

Body still. Breath natural. Mind at ease.

To extend your practice beyond yourself, bring to mind a person or a group of people, or a situation, whose suffering you would like to alleviate. Having brought them to mind, perhaps think:

> *By the power and truth of my meditation practice today, may all beings everywhere enjoy happiness and its causes, and may they be free from suffering and its causes.*

Now bring your awareness into your body, your entire body, as a composite whole. Feel for a few moments the physical sensations of your body. Notice if there is any tension in your face, shoulders, or belly, and relax.

Then, slowly scan your body and notice any tactile sensations. Feel first the parts of your body that are touching the floor. Notice the sensations on the bottom or sides of your feet, the sides of your ankles, and the sides of your knees. Just feel the sensations, and maybe notice if they are shifting or changing in any way.

Then feel your sit-bones pressing into your seat. Pressure, hardness, softness—whatever the sensations are, just notice them. Remain open and relaxed and attentive.

Then bring your attention to your straight spine. Slowly scan up your spine, over your sacrum, lower and mid-back, shoulders, and the back of your neck. Then spread your awareness over the back of your head, including behind your ears, and arrive at the top of your head. What sensations are you noticing? Vibrating, pulsating, buzzing, numbness? Whatever is happening, just notice it.

Now scan slowly down the front side of your body. Feel your forehead and temple region and examine the sinus region, moving into the head. If you feel any tension, relax and release.

Feel your eyes, cheeks, jaw, and lips. Assume a smile inside your mouth to relax your face and the back of your throat.

Moving down over your chin and chest, arrive in your belly region. Allow this to be loose and relaxed. There's no need to hold in any tension.

Now, staying in your belly region, turn your attention to your breath. Breathe naturally. Notice the movement in and out with each breath. Feel the sensations that come and go in your belly region while you are breathing. Allow your attention to remain here, observing the breath for a minute or so.

If the mind wanders off on a thought loop, no problem. Release the thinking, relax fully and with the rope of mindfulness, return to the practice. Release, relax, and return.

Next, move your attention to your chest and feel your breath. There's no need to name or think about what you sense. Rather, dive into

Mindfulness is only part of the story

Mindfulness has truly gone mainstream and is now being taught in schools, hospitals, and the corporate workplace. All kinds of media outlets, from *Time* and *Newsweek* to *The Guardian*, CNN, and the BBC, regularly report on the latest scientific research on the effects of mindfulness, and governments fund major research on the topic. Mindfulness courses are taught to young people in YMCAs, prisoners in state penitentiaries, and the world corporate élite at Davos. You can find mindfulness courses paired with nearly any activity, including "Mindfulness and Photography," "Mindfulness and Wine Tasting," "Intimate and Mindful Relationships" and even "Mindful Pet Care." There are slick mindfulness boutiques in capital cities, where you can pop in for wheatgrass shot before grabbing your mindful moment with noise-cancelling earphones. Super-star athletes talk about how mindfulness improves their performance on the court, while rock stars and actors tell us how it helps them relax from the stress of being a celebrity.

Jon Kabat-Zinn, Professor of Medicine Emeritus at the University of Massachusetts Medical School, is the individual who is most responsible for introducing mindfulness practice into the mainstream culture of the West, including hospitals and medical facilities. He writes:

> *Mindfulness practice means that we commit fully in each moment to be present; inviting ourselves to interface with this moment in full awareness, with the*

intention to embody as best we can an orientation of calmness, mindfulness, and equanimity right here and right now.

Mindfulness is a mental skill that anyone can develop and use in any situation, and I've no doubt that in some way it helps nearly everyone who brings it into their life. But I want to delve into this singular topic a little further here, so that we can place it properly within our overall practice of meditation, because it is only part of the story.

An antidote to distraction

First, let's remember the definition of mindfulness that Asanga gave us in the fourth century, which is "the non-forgetfulness of the mind with regard to a familiar object. Its function is non-distraction."

When applied to the practice of meditation, mindfulness is returning to our chosen object of concentration whenever we are distracted. We all know that when we sit down to meditate and focus on bodily sensations or the breath, our mind tends to do one of three things—either it is agitated and starts to think about something else, or it becomes bored and drops into lethargy, or it wants to sleep. Mindfulness counters all these tendencies. In other words, it is an antidote to distraction.

How does this antidote work? Mindfulness is effective because inherent within it is a specific plan of action:

- First, mindfulness remembers what the instructions are for the meditation practice, in our case to remain focused on our chosen object.

- Secondly, there is a kind of *abiding mindfulness* that binds the meditation instruction during the practice.

- And thirdly, there is a *prospective mindfulness* that knows, when distraction or dullness in the mind arises, to return to the practice.

This is the game plan for mindfulness and how it is an antidote to distraction.

Altruism and empathy

But there is more to our practice than just mindfulness. Remember that in the Buddhist and Hatha Yoga traditions, mindfulness and concentration were usually only taught to students after they had established a firm ethical and moral footing. The reason for this is that mindfulness practice, which leads to a pliable mind with single-pointed concentration abilities, is by itself neutral—neutral in the sense that a person can use it in any activity, including those that might be harmful.

To guard against our mindfulness and concentration skills being used to increase our anger, greed, or negative behavior, we adjust our attitude at the beginning of each session to remind ourselves that we are meditating not only for our own benefit but that so we might bring *intention to embody as best we can an orientation of calmness, mindfulness, and equanimity right here and right now.*

Mindfulness is a mental skill that anyone can develop and use in any situation, and I've no doubt that in some way it helps nearly everyone who brings it into their life. But I want to delve into this singular topic a little further here, so that we can place it properly within our overall practice of meditation, because it is only part of the story.

An antidote to distraction

First, let's remember the definition of mindfulness that Asanga gave us in the fourth century, which is "the non-forgetfulness of the mind with regard to a familiar object. Its function is non-distraction."

When applied to the practice of meditation, mindfulness is returning to our chosen object of concentration whenever we are distracted. We all know that when we sit down to meditate and focus on bodily sensations or the breath, our mind tends to do one of three things—either it is agitated and starts to think about something else, or it becomes bored and drops into lethargy, or it wants to sleep. Mindfulness counters all these tendencies. In other words, it is an antidote to distraction.

How does this antidote work? Mindfulness is effective because inherent within it is a specific plan of action:

- First, mindfulness remembers what the instructions are for the meditation practice, in our case to remain focused on our chosen object.

- Secondly, there is a kind of *abiding mindfulness* that binds the meditation instruction during the practice.

- And thirdly, there is a *prospective mindfulness* that knows, when distraction or dullness in the mind arises, to return to the practice.

This is the game plan for mindfulness and how it is an antidote to distraction.

Altruism and empathy

But there is more to our practice than just mindfulness. Remember that in the Buddhist and Hatha Yoga traditions, mindfulness and concentration were usually only taught to students after they had established a firm ethical and moral footing. The reason for this is that mindfulness practice, which leads to a pliable mind with single-pointed concentration abilities, is by itself neutral—neutral in the sense that a person can use it in any activity, including those that might be harmful.

To guard against our mindfulness and concentration skills being used to increase our anger, greed, or negative behavior, we adjust our attitude at the beginning of each session to remind ourselves that we are meditating not only for our own benefit but that so we might bring more love and compassion into the world. And, at the end, we direct the positive energy from our practice to the welfare of others through our dedication.

Through repeatedly recalling our motivation and dedication, we are training our mind in altruism and empathy. This moves our mindfulness practice in the direction of, as the Buddha called it, "right mindfulness"— mindfulness that leads towards compassionate action.

Guided meditation: Relaxed and alert with the breath

Find a comfortable and stable meditation posture. You can sit on the floor or a chair, or lie down. If you are sitting on the ground, steady your hips and legs. If you are in a chair, have your feet flat on the floor. If you are lying down, bend your knees and place your feet flat, or extend your legs with your feet falling away from each other.

In whatever posture you are meditating, find steadiness and comfort. Allow your spine to be straight, your shoulders pulled back and relaxed down, your chin slightly tucked under, the tip of your tongue touching or pointing toward your upper palate, and your eyes gently closed or half-open with a downward gaze.

Body like a mountain, majestic and steady.

Breath like the ocean, natural and vast.

Mind like the sky, clear and open.

Find balance in silence, stillness, and awareness.

Now, having found your motionless posture, you can establish your motivation for this session, perhaps thinking:

> *May my efforts today at meditation open my heart and mind*
> *so that I may understand and more skillfully help others in my*
> *family, my community and beyond.*

To start, inhale deeply and exhale completely. Just take a few breaths like this and then allow your breath to return to its natural flow.

Gather your mind and bring it into your body. Feel the physical sensations of your body sitting (or lying) still for a few moments. Feel the weight and steadiness of your foundation—whatever is touching the floor. Feel your spine extending upward from your foundation.

Then slowly sweep your attention down the front side of your body, relaxing your face, jaw, shoulders, chest, and belly.

Rest in stillness and feel the sensations of your body for another minute or so.

Then turn your attention to your breath. Locate where you feel it is strongest, perhaps in your nostril or lip region, or chest or belly. Wherever you feel it is most prominent, concentrate your attention there for this session.

Follow the full extent of the inhalation, the slight pause, and the full extent of the exhalation. Once again, dive into everything that is happening with your breath—the texture, temperature, and sensations. Does your breath have a scent or a taste? Follow it into your body and experience it fully.

When your mind moves away from concentrating on your breath, release whatever you are thinking about, relax deeply, and return to the practice.

If you have a running commentary in your mind about the meditation practice, release that voice as well. Every time you release and relax, you are being kind to yourself.

As you continue to follow your breath, on the inhalation, exert a bit more effort to concentrate on the totality of the breath. Focus on it a bit more strongly.

On the exhalation, release and relax, letting go of almost all mental effort.

Then repeat the pattern. On the inhalation, concentrate a bit more strongly; on the exhalation, relax more deeply. Alert, alert. Relax, relax.

Practice in this manner for 10 minutes or longer.

To conclude your meditation, on an exhalation, release and relax. Let go of any and all mental effort, including any idea that you are meditating. Simply remain there with an open presence.

To seal your meditation practice in an auspicious way, perhaps bring to mind a person or a group of people, or a place in the world where there is suffering, and think:

May my efforts today at meditation ripple into the world, bringing waves of peace, love, and joy to every being, near and far.

Chapter 4

Opening Completely to Our World

In meditation we are coming to know our mind because it is there that we experience happiness and suffering. As the Dalai Lama wrote in *The Art of Happiness*:

> *In identifying one's mental state as the prime factor in achieving happiness, of course that doesn't deny that our basic physical needs for food, clothing, and shelter must be met. But once these basic needs are met, the message is clear: we don't need more money, we don't need greater success or fame, we don't need the perfect body or even the perfect mate—right now, at this very moment, we have a mind, which is all the basic equipment we need to achieve complete happiness.*

Our mind is often clouded with turbulent thoughts and emotions that obscure us from seeing reality and having clear discernment in our life. But in our meditation training, we can see our experience as it is, rather than how we want, fear, or hope it to be.

The objects of our five senses

Now that we have some degree of concentration and mindfulness practice, we're going to open our meditation to our entire world by using objects of our five senses as the support for our practice. These are:

- touch

- sounds

- sights

- scents

- tastes

The method is the same as when we focused on tactile sensations during body scanning: we direct our awareness lightly toward a chosen object of our five senses and observe in a witnessing mode of direct perception.

We need not react to any of the sense objects, either by trying to prolong the experience or cut it short. Instead, we keep our awareness open and steady, and perceive whatever is presented to it. Most of us will, however, quickly observe how our mind wants to engage with certain forms of stimulation and tries to stop others. Take for example, a sound that you don't particularly like—the stomping of feet in the apartment above you, the sound of a leaf blower, or the roar of a motorcycle. The moment after that sound is perceived, you may react with displeasure, and a mental commentary quickly ensues about why the sound should stop, or perhaps anger or frustration swells up within you toward the individual making the sound. Another layer of mental commentary rapidly picks up to reinforce your dislike, and soon you're completely lost in a chain of thoughts, even when the original sound is no longer present. You are reacting to your reaction of the sound more than to the sound itself.

Take another example, such as an aroma you like, say that of freshly baked bread, or coffee, or pizza. Your awareness perceives that scent and a moment afterwards a sense of pleasure arises, which moves you to think about, perhaps, the last time you had that delicacy, or maybe move into the future to think, *Maybe I'll have pizza for lunch tomorrow ... and perhaps my best friend can join me to dine outside at the Italian café ... but oh no, I've heard there is snow forecast ... but how could there be snow in April ... for sure, I should try to support that environmental group that works on climate change.*

Wow! That was a quick succession of thoughts, almost effortlessly going from pizza to climate change! And we go on thinking excursions like this all day. Thought loop after thought loop after thought loop... Why do we do this? We do it because of our habit of thinking, and because of our attachment to some thoughts and aversion to other thoughts. Often the things we think about the most are those things for which we have a sincere dislike!

Is all of this thinking bad? What's the problem with allowing your mind to run off here and there? You should examine this question, and perhaps write about it in your meditation journal.

My point is that none of our thinking, conceptualizing, ruminating, and endless forays into the future or the past lead us to any lasting contentment. In fact, we are in an ever-revolving chase for some "thing" that will give us a degree of contentment, happiness, or wellbeing. When we do find things that give us moments of contentment, they seem to dissolve and we are left chasing again. This endless chasing creates an undercurrent of dis-ease in our life.

This is why we've been exploring what happens when we allow our chasing mind to settle a bit. When that happens, instead of chasing what we think will bring us happiness, we begin to experience what our life is really offering right now.

Using objects of the five senses in our meditation practice cultivates a relaxed and supple mind that isn't swayed by the objects around us. We needn't push away the objects of our senses, nor indulge in thinking about them either. In fact, what we are opening ourselves to is the complete experience of our life right now, in this body, with these senses.

In our next guided meditation practice we will begin by using sound as the object of our concentration.

Guided meditation: Sound

Assume your meditation posture. Arrange a solid foundation for your legs and hips. If you are seated, place a pillow or support under your backside and thighs, so that you feel completely supported. You can also lie down. In either case, have your spine straight, shoulders pulled back and relaxed, chin slightly tucked under, and your eyes either closed or open with a soft downward gaze.

Relax your body and bring your mind into your body.

Take a few deep breaths—a full inhalation all the way up to your collarbones and a deep relaxing exhalation. After a few breaths like this, allow your breathing to return to its natural flow.

To establish your motivation, perhaps think:

May this meditation practice bring a clarity of mind and openness to my heart, so that I may be more open, loving, and caring with my family, friends, and even those whom I do not know.

Settle your body into a posture of ease and let it rest there, stable and calm, including your eyes. Deeply relax. And turn your attention to feeling your body abiding in motionlessness.

Feel your legs for a few moments. What are the sensations there? Heaviness, groundedness, firmness?

Feel your spine's lift and notice any sensations along your back and the back of your head. Scan upwards.

Then slowly sweep your attention down the front side of your body, noticing the felt experience in your face, chest, and belly. Release any tension. Allow your abdomen to remain loose and relaxed.

Now turn your attention to the sounds around you. What sounds do you hear?

Perhaps the humming of any electrical appliances in the room or maybe a distant roar of an airplane in the sky. Perhaps you can hear the sound of your breath, or something else within your body. Open your awareness and take in any and all sounds, not focusing on or favoring any one in particular. Just listen.

There are likely to be many different sounds around you. Allow yourself to be aware of whatever sounds are more prominent.

You need not think about the sounds, or even name them. Nor attend to any mental images or ideas about them. Simply hear sound, any sound, for however long it lasts, and remain open to whatever sounds arise and fade away. Leave the hearing in the hearing, free of after-thinking and mental commentary.

You may also notice other things around you, such as sights or tactile sensations. This is no problem, but attend primarily to sound. Immerse yourself in the soundscape in a very relaxed and attentive way.

Let your awareness remain motionless, just aware of sound. Relaxed but not spaced out. Alert but not tense.

Practice in this manner for 10 minutes or so.

Finally, release your mental focus on sound and completely relax. Rest with an open presence for a short while.

To conclude with a dedication, perhaps you can think:

> *May my meditation practice today on sound bring spaciousness and clarity in my life so that I can more effectively benefit others.*

Be sure to write in your meditation journal about your first times practicing sound meditation.

We will meditate upon objects of all the five senses in our next session, but first I would like to discuss an important topic. We have been refining certain mental tools in our meditation practice, namely concentration, mindfulness, and relaxation. We have also talked about awareness, which I'd like to explore a little more deeply now.

What is awareness?

Often when we speak of awareness, we talk about awareness of some "thing," either one of the objects of touch, sound, sight, smell, and taste, or a mental object like an emotion or thought, for example, *I'm aware of the dog* or *I'm aware of how angry I am*. I'm not talking about the objects that awareness is aware of here. Rather, I'm talking about awareness itself—*that which knows, which perceives, which cognizes*.

Let's investigate this by looking at the qualities of awareness.

Illumination

First, awareness seems to illuminate any and all phenomena in our life. It is a kind of clarity that allows the entirety of our world to unfold in its manifest forms. So, in this sense, awareness illuminates.

An example of this that is often given by teachers in India is that of an old-time movie projector. I've heard this metaphor given by teachers in both the Buddhist and Hatha Yoga traditions as a way of thinking about the illuminating aspect of awareness.

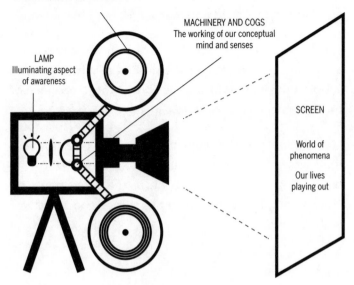

FILM
Our habitual tendencies, stories,
fuel for the cinema of our lives

MACHINERY AND COGS
The working of our conceptual
mind and senses

LAMP
Illuminating aspect
of awareness

SCREEN

World of
phenomena

Our lives
playing out

The process of illumination

When a movie is played, the images are projected onto a screen. That screen is like our world of phenomena, in which the drama of our life and the lives of those around us is being played out. These stories, outside us and even inside our head, are an enticing saga in which we often completely lose ourselves.

Then there is the filmstrip that moves through the projector. This film represents our habitual tendencies, likes, dislikes, and inclinations—the fuel for the narrative we tell ourselves about who we are and what we think and feel about the drama of our life.

The cogs, wheels, and machinery of the projector are like all of our different senses, which function to supply the appearance of a solid and real world upon the screen.

The screen, the film, and the projector are all creating appearances, but behind them all is a light bulb that supplies the light. Without the light of the lamp, none of the appearances would appear.

This light is like the illuminating aspect of awareness that allows the movie of our life to appear. While the drama depends upon the light, at the same time, the light is completely free of all the stories and narratives in the drama.

Cognizance

The second quality of awareness is knowing, or cognizance. Awareness not only illuminates, it also knows. Knows what? Whatever objects of the five physical senses and mental phenomena move before it.

Here the example of a mirror is often given. When an object moves in front of a mirror, the mirror reflects it exactly as it is, without changing, altering, or manipulating it. The mirror, or awareness, doesn't have to make an effort to perceive the object—it just happens.

When our awareness perceives an object, for the very first moment it does so purely, free of concepts, seeing it exactly as it is, just as a mirror effortlessly reflects an object. But the next moment, if our perception is affected by like or dislike, attachment or aversion, we tarnish that pure perception with our habit of labeling, then thinking, and the chain reaction of our thought loops. This "thinking" obscures the pure perception and we do not discern reality as it is, but rather as we think it is. In meditation we allow our awareness to remain in this mirror-like purity rather than obscuring it.

Returning to pure awareness

Is there ever a time when our awareness isn't functioning? Its illuminating and knowing aspects seem to be ever-present. Even when we're asleep and dreaming, it is this awareness that both illuminates our dreams and knows that they are happening.

Just as when we are dreaming but believe it to be real, so too in our waking state we get lost believing in the drama of our life. We become exhausted chasing contentment in our thought loops, because we can never quite find it there. We only meet dissatisfaction when we search for lasting contentment in our projections and thinking.

So what happens when we return, again and again, to pure knowing, to the illuminated awareness of *now*, instead of our habit of thinking? This is what we discover in meditation.

Transforming distraction into meditation

We have seen in our practice of focusing on tactile sensations, as well as sound, how we have a choice between observing directly what we experience, or being distracted by our mental habits of liking and disliking. Whereas before we started to meditate, the objects of our five senses—sensations, sounds, sights, scents and tastes—would send us off on thought loops, some short and some long in duration, now we are seeing for ourselves how sense objects that once were a cause of distraction are now integral to our meditation practice. We see how our distracted mind is a reminder to come back to the present, to return to the here and now.

Once I was with the Zen teacher Thich Nhat Hanh at his monastery in Thailand. We were sitting in an open-air meditation hall. Between the hall and the nearby rice paddy fields there was a large pond that was full of slimy green and brown mud.

I had come to meet Thich Nhat Hanh and discuss with him the challenges of being a meditator while still engaging in the world of social action, as his life had been an example of socially engaged Buddhism for more than 40 years. I told him how many young people who were involved in social change burned out quickly because they felt overwhelmed emotionally and couldn't sustain the energy needed to make a difference over the long haul. It was often their anger that tired them the most. And I asked him how he could view his so-called adversaries or political opponents with anything but aversion.

"How do you not let your anger overwhelm your composure and patience?"

He paused. Then he pointed toward that slimly green pond.

"There, you see?"

There was a single pure white lotus flower.

"No mud, no lotus."

That was all he said. *No mud, no lotus.* Then he rang a bell in front of him that signaled for us to meditate for a short while.

After we had meditated, he spoke again and equated three things: the lotus, the Buddha, and our potential for awakening. The lotus lives within the sludge of a dirty swamp, but is not tainted by it. Similarly, while the Buddha lived within the world of aggression and suffering, it was his compassion that blossomed.

And, just like the lotus and the Buddha, we too must rise to the challenge of meeting our distractions and aggravations—our own mud—with pristine awareness shining and compassion radiating.

Opening to all five senses

Any object of our five senses can be used individually in our meditation practice, just as we did with sound. Or, as we will now see, we can open all five senses up simultaneously.

In the practice, as before, we directly perceive an object as it appears to our awareness.

- *Sensation:* When we feel a sensation, we simply feel without needing to have an internal commentator interpret it for us. We don't even have to name or label it. Nor do we need to change or alter what we feel. We just feel the sensation.

- *Sound:* When there is sound, we allow our awareness to be open and spacious and we hear whatever sound moves to us or through us. Whatever it is, we simply hear it. And we leave the hearing in the hearing. We need not try to hear anything in particular or to stretch our hearing. We stay steady and merely hear whatever there is to be heard. And we continue as one sound fades and another arises.

- *Sight:* When we open our attention to visual stimulation, we observe without discursive thoughts, the colors, patterns, shapes, lightness and darkness, and whatever appears to our vision. Whether our eyes are open or closed doesn't really matter, although I recommend meditating with your eyes open. But in either case, we watch, we witness, and we observe the visual stimulation. And we leave the seeing in the seeing.

- *Scent:* When we open our awareness to our olfactory senses, we simply notice whatever scents are present—pungent, smoky, fruity, chemical, sweet, decayed, or fragrant. Again, we don't have to try to find scents. We just allow our awareness to know whatever scents are present.

- *Taste:* As for taste, we observe what tastes are on our palate—sweet, bitter, sour, or salty. We investigate the front of our tongue, our mid-mouth, and the back of our palate. We don't have to name the tastes, just directly experience them.

The Buddha taught this practice concisely in the *Root Sequence Discourse* (*Mulapariyaya Sutta*), when he said:

> *In what is seen, there should be just the seen;*
> *In what is heard, there should be just the heard;*
> *In what is felt, there should be just the felt;*
> *In what is known, there should be just the known.*

We will meditate upon the five senses sequentially, opening our attention to each sense field one by one, and then we will remain with all five of the senses open at once, spacious and attentive to whatever in the realm of the five senses presents itself to our awareness.

As for what we are to do if and when we get distracted: we notice, we release the thinking, relax, and return to the practice.

Guided meditation: All five senses

Find a comfortable place where you can sit or lie down and remain motionless for 10–15 minutes. Arrange your hips and legs so that you are steady and stable. Lengthen your spine, draw your shoulders back and down, and then relax. Slightly tuck your chin under as you relax your face. Release any gripping or tension around your eyes, at the back of your throat, in your shoulders or in your belly. Let your eyes be soft and closed, or, if open, in a downward gaze, resting motionless.

Having adjusted your posture, you can adjust your attitude to think:

> Through my practice of meditation today on the five senses, may I open my heart and mind completely so that I may be able to benefit more beings.

Gather your mind and bring it into your body. Feel your body as a composite whole, motionless.

Direct your awareness to hover within your body and feel whatever are the most prominent tactile sensations. Remain very relaxed, very alert. There's no need to think about the sensations. Just feel them. Lightness, heaviness, warmth, coolness—feel whatever sensations are present.

You may also notice that the sensations change as you perceive them. They may be pulsating, vibrating, or throbbing. Just notice them. You may also notice a kind of like or dislike of them. Just notice that too.

Stay with the sensations for a few minutes.

Now move the attention that has been on tactile sensation to the field of sound. You don't have to go here and there and try to find sounds, just let your awareness be open and still, and know whatever sounds are moving around you or through you. Perhaps you hear the thumping of your heart, or the rasping of your breath, or the humming of an air conditioner.

Some sounds move quickly, like cars swooshing by; others remain or repeat like the percussion of a ticking clock. Whatever is present, leave the hearing in the hearing. Listen, free of after-thinking.

Practice in this manner for a few minutes.

If you notice your mind moving away from your object or field of concentration, release the thinking, relax, and come back to the practice. No mud, no lotus.

Then, while leaving the doors to your previous two sense doors open, move your attention to the field of visual stimulation. Whether your eyes are closed or open, adopt a witnessing mode in perceiving whatever shapes, colors, patterns, or shades of light are presenting themselves to you.

Leave the seeing in the seeing. Observe whatever sights are present, free of after-thinking.

Practice like this for a few minutes.

Next, while leaving the doors to your previous three sense perceptions open, redirect your attention to whatever scents are around you. Notice whatever sweet, pungent, smoky, fruity, chemical, decayed, or fragrant scents are there. There's no need to name or label them. Simply smell them.

There may be a change present as one scent comes and goes, while others seem to persist. Perhaps you notice that you like or dislike different scents. There's no need to mentally push away or indulge. Just smell for a few minutes.

Turn your attention now to whatever tastes are present on your palate. Place your awareness on the front of your tongue, mid-tongue, and the back of the mouth. Notice the sweet, bitter, sour or salty tastes. Some might bring a kind of liking and some a kind of disliking. Just observe.

You don't have to think how the tastes got there. Just notice them.

Now allow all five of your senses to be completely open at once. Let your awareness be both vast and clear like the sky. Allow all of the objects of your five senses to be perceived purely, free of after-thinking. Sensations, sounds, sights, scents and tastes arise and dissolve.

Let your awareness be open and still and simply know whatever moves before it. There's no need to suppress or ignore any sense object, or indulge or think about it. Stay very relaxed. Very alert.

Practice like this for a few minutes.

Finally, let all mental effort go and relax. There's no need to concentrate now, or attend to anything, or use mindfulness. Release and relax in silent stillness for a few moments.

To conclude with an auspicious dedication, perhaps you can think:

> *By opening my mind and heart completely, may I discern*
> *clearly the way to be of most benefit to others.*

How to deal with strong emotions and 'experiences' during meditation

When we cultivate a calm body and mind in meditation as well as develop some degree of single-pointed concentration, it's not uncommon to have powerful surges of energy. Sometimes we experience these as strongly felt emotions. For individuals who have a strong visual disposition, there may be some kind of visionary experience. I'm not going to suggest an interpretation of any of these experiences. But I will offer this: if or when strong surges of energy seem to disrupt your meditation, you don't need to be particularly surprised, distressed, or elated.

What are you to do with these rather powerful experiences? In the context of the meditation practice presented thus far, the instruction is simply to return to the method: treat the strong surge of energy, emotion, or vision as any other cloud-like movement that arises and dissolves in the sky-like space of your awareness.

You might ask, "Shouldn't I figure out what these experiences mean during my meditation?"

If you want to investigate various kinds of meditation experiences through intellectual inquiry, you will have ample time to do so after your meditation practice concludes. But as far as formal meditation practice goes, the intent is to calm the body and mind and cultivate a non-distracted and attentive awareness that is not swayed by whatever emotions or visions or energies arise.

Once when I was on a strict Vipassana meditation retreat for a few weeks in Nepal, I had the very powerful feeling that I was levitating. We were practicing body scanning over and over during our 90-minute meditation sessions and each day we were meditating for 10 sessions, so it was rather intense. We were encouraged not to open our eyes, or shift our legs from half-lotus, or move our hands from our lap. But on the third day, I began to feel as though I was meditating about six inches off the ground. I was sure I was actually levitating.

Then on the next day I not only felt that I was levitating, but also that I was rocking from left to right like a pendulum.

I continued the meditation method, though I was nearly certain that what I was feeling was actually happening. It was quite exciting. I remembered reading stories of great yogis who could levitate and I thought that this experience must signify that I was on the precipice of grand meditative realizations!

After five consecutive days of having these feelings of levitating and swaying while I was meditating, I decided to ask a senior instructor about it. I described my experience to her, half-expecting a congratulatory response.

She grinned slightly and said in a matter of fact way, "Just open your eyes. See for yourself."

Sometimes reality checks come in the most painfully obvious ways!

Bliss, clarity and no-thought

There is one other point I'd like to mention regarding experiences during our meditation practice. Some meditation manuals I have studied refer to three kinds of experiences that indicate we are making progress along the meditation path. These are bliss, clarity, and no-thought:

- Bliss is a powerfully felt bodily sensation, sometimes localized and other times felt throughout the entire body.

- Clarity is a very intense single-pointedness that is so focused on the sole object of concentration that all other phenomena around us become muted, sometimes for hours at a time.

- And the experience of no-thought is an extended period of time, from minutes to hours, where thoughts simply do not arise in the mind, thus no distracted thinking follows.

If these experiences emerge, and how frequently they happen, in meditation is dependent upon the disposition of the individual, and all three will not necessarily occur in every individual. Generally, we are more predisposed toward one of the three.

If and when they do come into our meditation practice, it is likely the result of having attained some degree of single-pointed concentration. However, it should be noted, there are many other signs of progress on the meditation path.

I mention bliss, clarity, and no-thought not because we are trying to have these experiences, but rather as a cautionary example. While these three experiences may be a sign that single-pointed concentration is improving, a warning is given in the meditation manuals. They caution that meditation-based experiences like bliss, clarity and no-thought can become obstacles on the path of the meditator, because they can have an alluring quality. That is to say, when they arise, we tend to grasp them, not wanting to let them go, and then desire to experience them again in our next meditation session. There can even be a sense of "waiting" for a certain kind of experience to arise in meditation. This is a deviation from the path of meditation.

So, while experiencing bliss, clarity, and no-thought is a positive sign, the instruction for our practice remains the same as before: remain attentively relaxed and observe as experiences arise and dissolve, without any fear of losing them or hope of their return. Recognize them as mere experiences and see their ephemeral quality, how they are almost dream-like.

"What if I feel bodily pain when I meditate?"

I related earlier my experience of lower back pain on one of my first meditation retreats and how meditation transformed my relationship to it. During that retreat, the entire notion of "pain" dissolved as I continued to focus lightly on the sensation over the course of a few days, and what remained was the direct experience of pulsating heat and coldness. I saw how the label of "pain" was additional and the many stories I'd told myself about the "pain" were veils that prevented me from experiencing the sensation as it really was. My stories were more about my fear of pain than what I was actually experiencing.

That was one specific episode, and in the course of my 23 years of meditating, I've observed all kinds of different bodily pain in meditation. I'm not suggesting that we should try to have painful experiences, or create bodily discomfort in order to meditate upon them. We need not do that. Pain will arise quite naturally over the course of time—this is a time-honored truth for all of us! But when pain arises in our meditation, it can be quite instructive. It gives us the chance to observe our mental habits very precisely. This is to say, when we have an experience of, for example, throbbing, pulsating, or stabbing, we may sense it as unpleasant. Almost simultaneously, out of habit, we label it "pain" and want to get rid of it, mentally pushing it away, moving our body, and thinking about how not to have that feeling. Often, fear arises that the pain will never go away, making the entire experience even more unbearable *in our mind*. We fuel a chain reaction of thoughts and thinking that can make us feel uneasier mentally than the unpleasant sensation causing it.

I'm not saying pain isn't real, or that we should somehow convince ourselves not to address the physical maladies with which it is associated. What I'm proposing is that pain presents us with a chance to look at our mind, our perception, and our habitual reactions toward felt sensations.

Medical research in the last decade has indicated that mindfulness and meditation contribute positively to pain management, including in chronic pain sufferers. Much of the research has focused on the patients' perceived pain control, as well as depression arising from having chronic pain. If you are a chronic pain sufferer, I recommend that you speak to your doctor about incorporating mindfulness and meditation into your treatment.

What are we to do when pain arises in our body during meditation? We observe it. We look at it. If it is the kind of pain that requires us to move our body—say, for example, if our knee is aching badly—then we move. But if we don't need to move, we can use the opportunity to look deeply at the sensation, and at the same time watch what our mind does with it.

In watching the sensation, we may notice the actual feeling, rather than what we *think* about the feeling. This is an excellent opportunity to see the difference between what we actually experience and what we think about it. We are looking into how the present moment is, rather than how we want it to be.

We might see that the sensation is not a solid thing, a static state, but fluid, moving, a beating experience, full of change—and this is a precious time. See, we can know intellectually that everything changes, but when we experience change within our body, it is no longer in the realm of the intellect but in the realm of our experience-based knowledge. This leads directly to coming to know reality, because we are observing the ever-changing flow that we call the present.

We don't have to focus strongly on the sensations, rather approach them with the same spacious disposition that we always bring to our meditation practice. We observe, watch, and notice, attentively relaxed.

Caution! How not to become an escape artist from your life

When I practice and share meditation with others, I don't mind if there are ticking clocks, barking dogs, or street traffic around. Even busy places such as airports, where there is an avalanche of stimulation, can be wonderful locations for meditation. We don't have to react to the sights and sounds and other commotion around us; meditation is dependent upon our mind and our mental agility to give ourselves space not to react.

That said, meditation teachers and most of the retreat manuals I've studied recommend finding a location for formal meditation sessions or retreat that is free from the usual noises and distractions of everyday life.

This is especially helpful when we are establishing our meditation practice.

If you are fortunate to have a quiet place in your home, or can spend some time in a cabin in the mountains or by the ocean, by all means take advantage of that for your meditation practice. But again, I have to remind you that we practice meditation so that we can be *in the world fully* and not shy away from it. We don't want to use meditation practice, whether at home or in retreat, as an excuse to be an escape artist from our life! We should develop our meditation practice so that it is not dependent upon having the perfect external circumstance. Eventually, we will find that we can meditate anywhere, anytime.

Once I took a month away from my work as a human rights monitor to study and practice with my teacher in Tibet, and when I arrived he could tell I was in a stressful state. I told him about my work reporting on human rights violations and how angry I felt toward the perpetrators of the atrocities that I'd researched.

He nodded, but didn't say anything.

He was teaching me a meditation practice in retreat that cultivated profound tranquility in body and mind, and after a few days, my mind began to settle.

During the second week, however, he saw me becoming too comfortable and peaceful in my meditation practice and thought I might become attached to being calm. One morning while I was quietly meditating next to him, all of sudden he blurted out the names of the political leaders to whom I had a strong aversion.

I immediately reacted, feeling a kind of hot rage rise within my chest.

He saw this play out in me and said, "Watch your reactions, don't feed them. And then return to your object of concentration."

Chapter 5

Integrating Meditation into Everyday Life

Many of my friends tell me, "I want to meditate, but I find that I'm too busy with my life." I've heard countless times, "I'm just too busy to meditate."

Having lived in London, Kathmandu, New York City, and Washington, DC, I can very much relate to this sense of being overwhelmed by life, particularly in urban settings, and feeling as though there is little time to meditate. If you have this feeling but still want to establish a meditation practice, let me offer a few suggestions.

Develop an interest in meditation

First, if meditation is yet another task that you must place on your daily 'to do' list, another activity that you are doing because you've been told it's good for you, perhaps it's best not to meditate. If you have a sense of anxiety about your meditation practice, it's likely that the resilience required to sustain it really won't be there.

However, developing a strong daily meditation practice may simply be matter of making a slight adjustment to your attitude about meditation. Perhaps you can look at meditation as a discovery process that you approach with inquisitiveness and joy, rather than the heaviness of a duty or task.

Some of us spend an incredible amount of time taking care of our body with exercise—thousands of hours each year. We read about the exercise that is good for our body, we plan our day and week around our workouts and yoga and spinning classes, and then we execute our plan to be fit. Others spend an equal or more amount of time shopping for healthy food, researching the latest super-food, and preparing elaborate meals and organic smoothies. And when we aren't exercising or eating, we're scrolling our social media feed, where we find all sorts of temptations—places to vacation, clothes to buy, people to be like—all with the promise of some kind of lasting happiness.

There's nothing inherently negative about staying fit, eating well, going on vacation, and keeping in touch with others. But what we should recognize is that for those of us who have the luxury of looking after our fitness, eating whatever we want, and spending time on Facebook or Instagram, what we choose to spend our time doing indicates our priorities.

I heard a Tibetan meditation teacher in Kathmandu once tell a group of college students, "If you say you have no time to meditate, it means you have no interest in it. You can stand in line for four hours to buy a new iPhone, but you can't find 30 minutes to meditate! You are interested in your smartphone, so you find the time for it."

So, perhaps if you develop a little bit of interest in meditation, and understand the benefits of practicing it, you will prioritize the time for meditation.

I provided several suggestions earlier in the book for establishing a daily meditation practice (*see page 45*). However, if your duties at home or work get to be too much and you don't find the time for a formal session, don't feel bad about it. You'll find there are always natural "gaps" during the day when you can meditate, perhaps as you're waiting for the water to boil for your morning tea, or for your coffee to cool. Take those five to 10 minutes to sit silently and still and gather your intention and meditate for a short while.

Perhaps you can write in your meditation journal where these natural gaps occur during the course of your day—gaps where you can enliven your mind and refresh your attention with meditation.

The spontaneous and informal session

Here's another suggestion—the moment you think, *I should meditate*, or *I should really be meditating more often*, there and then, meditate. Direct your attention to the sensations of your body if you are seated, or even walking. Scan your body or perhaps transition to watching your breath for a few minutes. Just gather your attention, relax, and find freedom in your meditation practice.

You can do this on the bus or train, while waiting for an appointment or flight, or any number of times when you often allow your mind to wander. Otherwise you may habitually fill the time and space with scrolling your social media feed, reading endless emails, or flipping through a magazine.

If you're at work, just take a moment in your office chair. You needn't do anything except turn your mind inward, feel your body, locate your breath, and relax with a light focus on a chosen object. It can be that simple. And powerful. No need for anyone to know you are meditating! It's probably best, however, not to meditate if your attention is needed elsewhere—like driving.

Find your "go-to" practice that you can rely upon anytime, anywhere. My go-to practice is breathing meditation— inhaling with attention, exhaling with relaxation. Don't think that you have to have your meditation cushion, a totally quiet room with incense burning and a candle lit! These are nice supports for meditation practice. But if you wait until you have all the conditions ready before you meditate, you'll miss opportunities to practice.

Meditating and being mindfully aware aren't so much what you do, but who you are. So, try to make time to have formal meditation sessions, but remember that spontaneous and informal sessions are a skillful way to integrate meditation into your daily life.

Let's take a look at one such practice off the cushion—walking meditation.

Walking meditation

Walking meditation is an excellent and accessible way of practicing mindfulness awareness. You can think of it as a link between a formal, seated meditation practice and informal daily life.

Thich Nhat Hanh wrote in *The Miracle of Mindfulness*:

> *People usually consider walking on water or in thin air a miracle. But I think the real miracle is not to walk either on water or in thin air, but to walk on earth. Every day we are engaged in a miracle which we don't even recognize: a blue sky, white clouds, green leaves, the black, curious eyes of a child—our own two eyes. All is a miracle.*

Walking meditation isn't complicated. Essentially, we are imbuing an action that we may do automatically with the mindfulness and awareness we have cultivated in our seated practice. It's good to do walking meditation if we are feeling lethargic in our body or foggy in our mind. Generally, walking meditation enlivens the mind.

Walking meditation can be practiced alone or in a group in a formal manner, especially if you have a room or a garden where there are not others moving here and there.

The practice is simply being present with what is happening in your body as you move. Be aware of the world around you—with some caution, responding as needed—but keep your primary focus on feeling your body, or perhaps only your feet. There's no need to watch your feet, though your gaze can be directed downward if that suits you. Thich Nhat Hanh encourages you to "Walk as if you are kissing the Earth with your feet."

For formal walking meditation practice, you can slowly walk for 10 minutes in a clockwise direction, or else back and forth for 20 or so paces and then turn around. Keep your body relaxed and your eyes softly gazing down as you walk mindfully and feel your body. Begin and end the formal sessions with a brief period of sitting meditation practice.

If you are practicing walking meditation in a public space, there's no need to walk slowly. You can practice when walking to the bus or metro, or casually walking in the park, or with your dog.

Try it for yourself with the following guided meditation.

Guided meditation: Walking

Let's begin in a seated posture. If you are at home it can be in the room where you will then walk, or if you are outside, perhaps on a park bench.

Sitting, rest for a few moments in stillness, eyes open in a downward gaze. Bring a light awareness to the sensations of your body, as you remain motionless.

Then, to establish your motivation, perhaps think:

> *I will practice mindfulness and awareness through walking meditation today so that I may be more fully present in all of my activities and able to benefit others.*

Now return your awareness to the sensations of your body. You might notice a heaviness or lightness in the legs, or pressure or relaxation in ankles, knees and hips. Notice how your spine feels, and your shoulders, as you relax your face.

Then, very mindfully, noticing the sensations, slowly stand up. Pausing momentarily, notice the felt experience of your body in a standing position. Let your awareness hover on whatever sensations are the strongest.

Your hands can be at your side, or you might like to make a soft fist with your right hand and place it in the palm of your left hand

and hold at your heart. Then, if you are in a public space, begin walking normally. If you are in your home or garden, walk slowly and deliberately in a clockwise direction or else back and forth.

As you move, feel the sensation of your feet and legs lifting through space. Notice the touching and sensations in your heel, mid-foot, and toes. Notice the transfer of weight, the balance forward and backward and side to side.

You don't have to visualize or think about or name each body part as you feel it, just feel the tactile sensation. Hardness. Softness. Movement.

Touching, what is the feeling? Lifting, what is the feeling?

If your mind begins to think about something, no problem. When you recognize that, just release the thinking, relax, and come back to the feeling of your feet touching the ground.

Continue to walk slowly if you are indoors, or if you are in a public space, at a normal pace.

Feel the temperature of the air on your face and arms.

Feel the steadiness of the ground.

Feel the movement of your feet, knees and hips.

Touch the ever-changing present.

After some time, you may return to your original seat, and slowly sit down. If you are in a public space, perhaps return to a park bench or take a seat on a bus.

As you take your seat, relax deeply and feel the sensation of a still body. Feel your body as a composite whole. Just notice whatever sensations are presenting themselves to your awareness. Remain relaxed and attentive.

To conclude, let go of any mental effort to be mindful and simply rest for a few minutes.

For your dedication, perhaps you can think:

> *Whoever sees me, hears me, or contacts me, may I be able to benefit them in order to make a more peaceful and harmonious world.*

Falling asleep

Many of us have difficulty falling asleep, or wake up in the middle of the night and can't get back to sleep. I've talked to many people who have described various challenges with sleeping. A common reason for not being able to fall asleep is because of racing thoughts and an inability to stop chasing after them. Some individuals have told me about how, when they can't fall asleep, they get frustrated with themselves and begin repetitive thought loops about why they can't fall asleep, which has the effect of waking up the mind rather than letting it rest.

Some recent somnology studies have indicated that a daily mindfulness practice leads to better sleep patterns, including being able fall asleep, and stay asleep, more easily. Many individuals I have meditated with benefit from a short meditation right before they fall asleep.

I would warn you, however, that meditation—in the manner that we have approached it in this book—can have the effect of waking up the mind. When people ask me for advice on meditating in order to sleep better, the following is what I recommend.

First, the reason individuals are unable to fall asleep, or stay asleep, may be the various activities that they are involved in while they are awake. So, for example, we should consider what we eat, the amount we eat, when we eat it and how it affects us. Similarly we have to see how our exercise, or lack thereof, contributes to our sleep. We also have to assess honestly if the amount of time we spend on computer or smartphone screens brings about a calm state of mind or agitates and upsets us. There are a whole host of lifestyle questions into which we need to look. We must not think that meditation is a panacea. Our life is an interdependent one, and many different causes and conditions can be disrupting our sleep.

With that said, and having read many medical studies on the benefits that mindfulness and meditation practice have on sleep quality, I recommend a daily meditation practice of 20 minutes following the methods I present in this book.

As for what to do right before bed, here's a suggestion:

Practice: Letting go before sleeping

Arrange yourself comfortably in bed, lying on your back under the blanket or duvet, with a pillow under your head, your arms at a 30-degree angle at your side with your palms facing up, your legs straight and your feet falling to the side.

Perhaps think:

May all beings everywhere find comfort, ease, and rest.

Then, to begin, feel your breath at your belly. Feel the inhalation and exhalation. And as you do so, allow your body to feel heavy.

Take a few full inhalations and relaxing exhalations, then, after a few rounds, let your breath return to its natural rhythm.

Allow your awareness to permeate your entire body. Feel your body relaxing more deeply with every out-breath.

Breathe out, releasing all thoughts and images and expectations, and then gently breathe in.

If your mind follows a thought, that's not a problem. When you notice it, release the thinking, relax, and return very gently to the breath. You may have to do this a few times. No problem.

With every out-breath, release and relax.

Return to the natural rhythm of your breath. Settle into it. Let your breath be soft and smooth.

Be lightly present as you settle into progressively deeper states of ease and release.

After a short while, you may notice a velvety quality to your mind, a soft, hazy feeling. This indicates the beginning of the transition to sleep.

Let go of watching the breath, trying to relax, or exerting any effort at all. Remain still, or roll onto your right side, and fall asleep in a smooth transition.

Drinking and eating like the Buddha

At first, meditation is coming to know our mind through the effort-filled practicing of formal meditation sessions. As we progress, though, we will find that mindfulness, awareness, spaciousness, responsiveness and the other qualities that arise from our practice are not so much something that we do, but rather what we become. In other words, the fruition of our practice and the practice itself become one.

To help with this process, let me suggest two different occasions when you can begin to incorporate mindfulness, concentration, spacious awareness, and other meditative qualities into your daily life. They are when you are drinking tea or coffee, and when you are taking your meals.

Often when we are doing these activities, our attention is on anything but the beverage or food. Instead, we are talking to people, either directly or on the phone, or listening to the radio or a podcast or television, or thinking about the future or wandering in daydreams. How often have we finished our tea or eaten half our meal before we have actually tasted what we have been putting in our mouth?

What is the practice then for drinking and eating? As we saw with our walking meditation, it is to be fully and completely present with the totality of the experience.

Here are two brief meditation practices for drinking tea and eating.

Guided meditation: Drinking tea

With the warm beverage in front of you, take a moment to ground yourself by noticing how your body feels. Is there anticipation or settledness as you sit with your cup of tea? Is your body relaxed or tense? What is happening on your palate at the moment?

As you notice your present state, straighten your spine and relax your face, shoulders, and belly.

You might consider the innumerable beings who have contributed to this cup of tea and then think:

> *Through the energy and comfort I receive from this tea, may I radiate love and compassion to all beings.*

Then turn your attention to the cup of tea in front of you. Notice the color and light on the cup and the tea. Watch the steam. Take in the array of visual stimulation that comes with the tea, and notice any reaction that may be stirred in your mind.

Taking the cup of tea in both hands, sense the warmth in your palms and smell the aroma in the front of your nose, the back of your throat, and your chest. Rest completely in the experience.

Finally, taste the tea, and feel the bursting of sensation on your tongue and through your mouth, the warmth descending as you swallow. Open completely to the experience of a sip of tea.

Setting the teacup down, leave all five of your senses wide open and experience the ever-changing flow of the present moment in its entirety.

Remember that Thich Nhat Hanh encourages us to:

> *Drink your tea slowly and reverently, as if it is the axis on which the world Earth revolves – slowly, evenly, without rushing toward the future; live the actual moment. Only this moment is life.*

Continue in this manner until you finish the cup of tea. Patiently savor every moment of drinking tea with your senses wide open.

After you have finished your tea, set the cup down in front of you and perhaps think:

> *May the vitality this cup of tea gives me be used to bring contentment to others in my family and my community.*

Guided meditation: Eating

You can incorporate the practice of mindfulness awareness into eating too. If you are with others, perhaps you can take the opportunity to eat a meal and share silence, which can be wonderful and provide a deep connection.

Whether you are along or with others, as you take your seat with a plate of food, generating gratitude, perhaps you can reflect:

> *There are an innumerable number of beings who have had some part in bringing this meal to me. May I repay their kindness in the world.*

Then briefly turn your attention to your body. Sitting still, with a comfortably straight spine, rest your body completely, allowing your face, shoulders and belly to relax.

Turn your attention to the plate of food and notice the colors and shapes on the plate. It's fine if the names of the food arise in your mind, but there's no need to think about them, just observe the visual stimulation.

Perhaps move your face over the plate and take in the various aromas of the food. Notice what is happening within you as you do so. Is it eagerness? Is there any sense of urgency?

Mindfully moving your hands and grasping the utensil(s), take your first bite. Feel the complex textures in your mouth, the chewing action, and the sensations when you swallow the food.

Pause and feel again the experience in its entirety. Continue mindfully eating in this manner until you have finished.

At the conclusion of your meal, dedicate your efforts to the wellbeing of others.

To supplement your practice, you might write in your meditation journal how you think the Buddha, or Jesus, or other individuals of deep wisdom and compassion might have taken their tea and meals.

Chapter 6

Working within Our Mind

My first Tibetan Buddhist meditation teacher often said things like, "Happiness and suffering come from your own mind, not from outside. Your own mind is the cause of happiness; your own mind is the cause of suffering. To obtain happiness and pacify suffering, you have to work within your own mind."

I've come to realize that meditation practice is all about dedicating ourselves to the "work within your own mind."

When we work within our mind, we find that it seems to have two aspects:

• There is the aspect of cognizance, or *pure knowing*, what we have called "awareness." I'm not referring to the brain, or neural patterns, here, rather that part of the mind that knows.

- And then there are the objects that appear to the mind, or *that which is known* by awareness, such as sights, sounds, and even thoughts. Sometimes people associate the mind with feelings or emotions. But these too are just what appears to the mind.

Distinguishing between the *knowing aspect* of mind and *what appears* to the mind is what we come to see and understand for ourselves in meditation.

Whatever moves through the mind is temporary and oftentimes fleeting. How long does a thought, an emotion or feeling remain in the mind? Or how long does the perception of one of the senses, like a sound, last in the mind?

Even though these ideas, thoughts, sensations, and desires are momentary, we often identify very closely with them and hold on to them for dear life. We have a habit of trying to grasp them, and then thinking about them, considering them the source of our contentment and happiness. But how can we find contentment and happiness in that which is so momentary and transient?

We give a lot of importance to appearances, especially to the stories that we narrate about those appearances—our thought loops, our long ruminations. We take them so seriously. We believe in them. We identify with them. We defend them. We act upon our thoughts about appearances, even when they don't accord with reality.

We can spend most of our life thinking about these "appearance" aspects of the mind without understanding that we are more than that. Not understanding the difference between the mind and that which appears in the mind is where we might find the beginning of our own confusion, or what is sometimes called "ignorance."

Our confusion is likened to the way that one may confuse a colored rope for a snake. The analogy goes something like this: say a man is walking on the grass in the evening and comes upon a coiled rope. Though it is a rope, he misperceives it and thinks it is a snake, jumps back, almost has a heart attack and runs to tell the neighbors that a dangerous snake is roaming the neighborhood. All the local children are locked in their homes, and then the media finds out and there are reports of a poisonous snake having almost eaten a child, so the police get involved, and so on.

Now, the scenario started with a two-fold problem. First, the man didn't see the rope for what it was; a rope. That was his first mistake—not seeing reality as it was. And then he made a second mistake by projecting "snake" upon the rope. He projected the label of "snake" where there was no basis for it. Then he reacted and the entire town was involved in the search for the non-existent snake.

How often during the course of the day do we make this two-fold mistake?

Fortunately, our meditation practice positions our mind to correct these faults and misperceptions.

In our next meditation practice, we're going to work within the mind itself. When we use the mind, and the appearances of the mind, in our meditation practice, the focus is not on trying to figure out, analyze, or even think about the reason for the arising of every thought, feeling, emotion, dream, desire, fear, or anything else that appears to the mind. Rather, the practice takes us to the very root of what awareness is, and by remaining in the pure awareness aspect of the mind, our thoughts, feelings, and emotions begin to lose the control that they once had.

In other words, we have a choice between engaging with our thoughts and emotions or not engaging.

A process of empowering ourselves through our own awareness takes place during this practice, because we see directly that the root of our contentment lies in our own mind.

For the meditation practice itself, we're going to use the spacious aspect of the mind, and that which moves through the mind, as the object of our focus.

How do we do this? As usual, we rest the body in stillness, then scan it briefly, and then turn our attention to the space where thoughts, emotions, and perhaps mental images move. We rest our attention in that space, and we observe whatever arises and dissolves in that space. We don't have to suppress anything because we're afraid we'll be distracted. Nor do we have to indulge any thought or emotion with thinking. We just observe the mental field of our experience in a relaxed and attentive manner.

Guided meditation: Mind

Assume your meditation posture, either seated on the floor, on a chair, or lying down. Rest your body in a stable position so that your feet, ankles, thighs, and hips are firmly arranged and create a steady foundation. Straighten and then relax your spine. Find a comfortable place for your hands in your lap or on your knees. Your eyes may be open with a downward gaze, looking into space, or gently closed.

Take a few deep inhalations and exhalations, pausing momentarily with your lungs completely full and then exhaling in a long and slow manner with your mouth open.

After a few rounds, let your breathing return to its natural flow.

To establish your motivation for today's meditation practice, perhaps think of a person, or people, or situation in need of material or emotional support, and think:

Through my efforts today in meditation, may all beings everywhere find comfort and ease in their mind.

Rest in stillness. Feel the motionlessness of your lower torso, and any other sensations. Feel the elongation of your spine. Scan all the way to the top of your head. And slowly sweep your attention down the front side of your body, relaxing your face, shoulders, and belly completely. Let your body remain immovable like a mountain.

Then focus the attention that was just noticing the sensations of your body and redirect it for a moment to notice any sounds around you. Then just leave them be.

Notice any visual stimulation. It doesn't matter whether your eyes are open or closed, just notice the shapes, colors, and shades of light.

And for a moment, notice what tastes are on your tongue, and what scents are around you.

Allow the world of your five senses around you to rise and fall. Keeping your body still, allow whatever is happening around you to come and go.

Then move your attention to the space where thoughts, thinking, emotions, ideas, and mental imagery move. It is a gentle turning inward of the mind.

Observe that space of the mind without suppressing any thoughts or indulging in thinking. Remain very relaxed, very alert. The object of your meditation practice is whatever arises in your mind in the immediacy of the ever-changing present moment.

There may be moments when there is nothing moving through your mind. Remain in the spacious clarity of that moment. Abide there.

Then, when thoughts, ideas, or emotions arise, watch them with complete openness. Like a hawk soaring through the sky without leaving a trail or wake behind it, allow them to move through the space of the mind leaving no trace.

As you continue to practice, be mindful that your attention doesn't sink or collapse into lethargy, where you may not be distracted, but not have attentive clarity. If this happens, straighten your spine and revive your meditation.

If you notice you have become distracted and are thinking about something else, release the thinking, relax, and return to the space where thoughts and emotions move. Rest your awareness there, spacious and alert.

After 20 minutes or so, let go of the method and rest in silent stillness for a few moments.

And to conclude the practice in an auspicious manner, perhaps you can think:

> *Through the power and the truth of my meditation practice today, may I empower myself to be a force for good and peace in the world.*

A map of distraction: the Eight Consciousnesses

Different religious and spiritual traditions offer a variety of theories, concepts, and maps to understand our journey inward. These maps of course are not the territory, but provide us with helpful clues and the general direction in which to proceed. One Buddhist map of the mind in particular, known as *the Eight Consciousnesses*, I find helpful because it is very practical for meditators. We can use this map to understand a critical junction in our meditation practice—that crossroad where we either rest in pure awareness (the knowing aspect of mind) or veer into distraction (our well-trodden thought loops).

The Eight Consciousnesses help us to sort out conceptually what is happening with the complicated process—what is happening within the mind itself during the perception of stimulation and subsequent reaction to it.

You actually already have a familiarity with the Eight Consciousnesses through your practice of meditation so far. Now let's look at each consciousness individually, and then how they work together.

The five consciousnesses: Where we experience the physical world

The first five consciousnesses within our mind function with a corresponding sense organ to perceive an object, and include:

1. Tactile consciousness that utilizes the body to feel touch.

2. Auditory consciousness that utilizes the ears to hear sound.

3. Visual consciousness that utilizes the eyes to see objects.

4. Olfactory consciousness that utilizes the nose to smell scents.

5. Gustatory consciousness that utilizes the tongue to taste.

The sixth consciousness: Where we experience the mental world

6. The mental consciousness utilizes the conceptual mind to perceive thoughts, emotions and mental images.

In our previous meditation practices, we concentrated on the objects of the six consciousnesses. For example, in our body-scanning and breath meditation practices, we relied primarily upon the tactile consciousness to be aware of touch. And in our meditation practice on all five sensory stimulation, we used the corresponding sense consciousness to know the various objects of our five senses. When we meditated upon thoughts and emotions, we relied upon the mental consciousness.

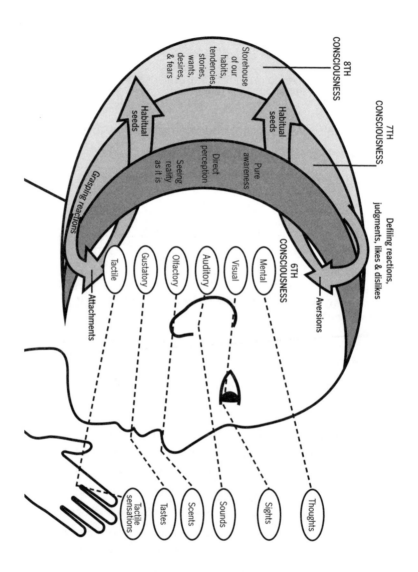

The eight consciousnesses

Regardless of which of the six consciousnesses we used, it was our *pure awareness* that perceived the object. So you could say that our pure awareness uses the six consciousnesses to know the world around us. Is there anything in our experience that is outside these six sense fields? It does not seem to me that there is.

Our perception of our physical surroundings and what is happening in our mind is marked by dynamism and fluidity. As we mentioned earlier, when our pure awareness perceives an object through one of the six consciousnesses, in the first moment of perception, it knows it exactly as it is, purely, just as a mirror reflects something perfectly as it is. For example, when our awareness, using our visual consciousness and eyes, sees a flower, for the first moment it does so with absolute clarity, even before the name "flower" or "rose" or "tulip" enters the mind. We just see the unique shape and color as it is right then and there. That is why I call it "pure" awareness.

Or, when our pure awareness uses our auditory consciousness and ears to hear a sound, our very first apprehension of that sound is a direct perception of it, before labeling, naming, or any other kind of thinking enters into the process.

With any phenomena of the six senses, when awareness apprehends an object, it does so in a pure, direct and unelaborate way, free of after-thinking or analysis.

The seventh consciousness: Where our pure awareness is defiled

If we were to abide continually in the direct perception of any and all objects as they unfolded to our awareness, then we wouldn't talk about the seventh consciousness. But do we actually do that in our meditation practice or in life in general? How often do we leave the hearing in the hearing, the seeing in the seeing, or allow thoughts to arise and dissolve without thinking about them? Most often, the moment after our pure awareness perceives an object, we either like or dislike the object; we want to hold it or we push it away, we identify with it or negate it. This is the instant when the seventh consciousness emerges, sometimes known as *the defiling consciousness*, because it spoils the pure perception of our awareness.

What spoils it? Our own habitual wants, desires, fears, and stories. These hijack our awareness's pure perception and lead it astray.

B. Alan Wallace suggests in *Minding Closely* that this spoiling of our awareness—in the seventh consciousness—is a kind of mental toxicity:

> *Toxic thoughts can ruin a day or a lifetime, but only if they are closely grasped. To the extent you can cultivate the ability of simply being present with whatever thoughts arise in the space of awareness— without grasping or aversion— thoughts lose their toxicity.*

Some teachers suggest the seventh consciousness is where our "self-cherishing ego" is fully manifest, or where our "grasping self" emerges. In any case, it is in the seventh consciousness that our repetitive thought loops begin, minute by minute, hour after hour, and continue day after day. And in this repetition, our mental habits are formed, molded, and reinforced, one thought loop at a time, in reaction to the stimulation of the six senses.

How many times a day do we drift on thought loops and reinforce our habits of attachments or aversion? A couple times a day, a dozen, or perhaps hundreds or thousands of times each and every day?

The eighth consciousness: Where we store our habits

The eighth consciousness is sometimes known as *the storehouse consciousness*, because it is here that our habits—our wants, desires, stories, and the like—are stored. The image of seeds being kept in a storehouse is often given, with each seed representing our habitual tendencies, our attractions and aversions, our likes and dislikes—all the fuel behind our self-cherishing ego.

Every time we react (seventh consciousness) to stimulation of the six consciousnesses, we are dropping more seeds into the eighth consciousness—stockpiling and reinforcing our habitual tendencies. We have seeds for the entire spectrum of our reactions stored here. It follows then that the eighth consciousness is the basis upon which the seventh consciousness arises.

How do we reverse the stockpiling and fortifying of habits in the eighth consciousness? Is it possible to empty the eight consciousness completely so that we can abide continuously in the pure awareness of whatever arises?

This is precisely why we meditate. We meditate to rid ourselves of our hang-ups, stories, and habitual tendencies to react. In other words, by continually resting in our pure perception, we can remove the force behind the seventh consciousness defiling our awareness.

When we remain keenly attentive of anything and everything that presents itself to our awareness but don't react mindlessly, we don't plant any more seeds in the eight consciousness. Every time we watch a thought move through our mind and we don't react, we are emptying the eighth consciousness of one seed, one story, one hang-up. This process is sometimes called *purifying the mind*, because we are removing the veils that obscure our pure awareness.

This explanation of the seventh and eighth consciousness resonates with a beautiful poem by the English playwright Noël Coward entitled *Nothing is Lost*, in which he suggests that in our subconscious (the eighth consciousness):

Lie all our memories, lie all the notes
Of all the music we have ever heard
And all the phrases those we loved have spoken...
Everything seen, experienced, each word...
Waiting to be recalled, waiting to rise.

It may seem as if we have no option but to be ruled by our habitual responses in our seventh consciousness. It may seem that we are pushed and pulled by our reactions to attachment and aversion all day long. But we don't have to succumb to the seventh consciousness, where we continually chase, but never find, contentment or ease. Through training in meditation and coming to know our mind, we understand that we do have the choice of remaining in our pure awareness.

Our practice therefore is to remain aware—with utter clarity and spacious relaxation—and not be pulled here and there by the seventh consciousness. And when we do venture into the seventh consciousness with our usual stories, the rope of mindfulness can pull us out and we can return to pure awareness of the ever-changing present moment.

The Dalai Lama's sandals

This may all sound rather theoretical and you may ask, "How is meditation relevant in daily life?" Of course only you can verify if practicing meditation brings benefits to you and is relevant in your life. You must study and learn the methods, exert mindfulness and energy in meditation, and examine if the results bring happiness, calmness, and concentration. And patience is required of course—the benefits do not come overnight.

Earlier I shared ways in which meditation practice has helped me understand my mind and mental habits, especially within the context of formal sitting practice. Now I want to tell you one specific way in which meditation has been directly applicable off the meditation cushion in my life as a writer.

Back in 2011, I published my first book, *In the Shadow of the Buddha*. It was a memoir of my decade-long pilgrimage in Tibet, during which I not only studied the life of a 19th-century mystic named Tertön Sogyal, but also documented human rights abuses and smuggled clandestine information out of various countries. When I completed the first draft of the book, I sent it to Gary Snyder, the American Beat poet, who had kindly offered to read and comment on it.

After a few months, I met him to discuss the draft. Gary Snyder is a Zen-monk-meets-American-lumberjack kind of character, very incisive, and quite stern. We met at a diner, and before coffee was served, he opened his bag and took out my manuscript. He pushed it toward me and I could see red marks all over the first chapter, where I'd written about meeting the Dalai Lama for first time in the 1990s.

In the draft, I'd written something like, "The Dalai Lama departed his residence and I was waiting there with many Tibetans. Tibetans consider the Dalai Lama to be the manifestation of compassion, known in Sanskrit as Avalokiteshvara, and in Tibetan as Chenrezig, who is iconographically depicted as the deity who has eleven heads and one thousand arms, each with the eye of wisdom in the hands..." and so forth.

Gary Snyder pointed to that passage and said, "Is that *really* what you were experiencing when you saw the Dalai Lama for the first time? Iconography and terms in Sanskrit and Tibetan?"

"I don't know. I can't remember," I said.

Snyder looked disappointed with my response. "But it's your *job* to remember!" he said gruffly. "What was the experience for you? Whether you are a meditator or a writer, or *just alive*, this is your responsibility: to know, to remember, to be aware of these things—because this is your reality. Recall it for me. Right now. What did it smell like? What were the sounds around you? What did your skin feel like? What did you actually see?"

As he asked the questions, the scene came back to me and I remembered what had actually happened.

"There was juniper incense burning," I recalled. "Monkeys were chattering in the trees above us. And actually I didn't see the Dalai Lama very well at all. When he exited his residence, the group of Tibetans behind me surged forward with devotion and pushed me forward too. In the crush, I found myself on my knees when the Dalai Lama walked by. So I didn't see him at all—or at least, all I saw was his sandals. And all I heard was his deep chuckle."

"Ahh," said Snyder, "then that is what you should write— juniper incense, monkey chatter, and the Dalai Lama's sandals and laughter."

There are very practical applications to bringing more mindfulness awareness into our life, as Snyder reminded me. I took his advice and rewrote the entire book.

How often during the day do we get lost in our thinking and miss what is readily before us? For example, when we meet our wife, husband or partner, or our children, do we actually hear what they are saying or do we hear what we are thinking about what they have said? Oftentimes, we only hear the commentary in our head rather than what the person in front of us is actually saying.

When I first started meditating I noticed immediately that I would often get lost in my mental projections rather than be present, for example when I'd meet a friend and have a kind of inner "comparison" commentary. How often do we see a friend or colleague, or even a stranger, and observe the totality of their presence instead of comparing some aspect of ourselves to them? How often do we allow our awareness to unfold and take in the ever-changing present instead of constricting our mind and being tightly bound by our thinking?

In coming to know our mind through meditation practice, we continue to be open to what is actually happening rather than the stories in our head.

Perhaps you can write down in your journal how your practice benefits you on and off your meditation cushion.

Advice on gaining flexibility, stability, and ease in your meditation posture

When we are working with our mind, we might find that while we want to meditate for longer periods of time, our body doesn't want to come along for the ride. So, learning some basic yoga postures, or exercises that focus on flexibility and mobility, can be very beneficial to our meditation practice. This is because yoga postures, stretching, and mobility training prepare the body to sit comfortably with ease and strength for extended periods of time.

Classic meditation postures include half- or full lotus pose (*padmasana*) and the adept's pose (*siddhasana*), as well as simply sitting on a chair.

Half- or full lotus pose (Padmasana)

The adept's pose (Siddhasana)

Chair posture

The most important aspect of your seated meditation posture is that it is steady and comfortable. Make sure your sit-bones are comfortably placed on the floor, cushion or seat, and your pelvis is neutral, i.e. you are neither arching your lower back nor collapsing backward. When your stable foundation is set, your spine falls into natural alignment with greater ease and comfort.

To increase flexibility and strength so that you can remain in physical ease in your meditation posture, take some time each day to sit in postures such as hero's pose (*virasana*), cobbler's pose (*baddhakonasana*), or squat pose (*malasana*).

Hero's pose (Virasana)

Cobbler's pose (Baddhakonasana)

Squat pose (Malasana)

These postures might be part of your daily yoga practice, but you can also sit in them when you are on your computer, eating, or doing other activities during the day.

Using support with blocks or blankets is highly recommended when assuming these postures, or when meditating. With the right preparation and some regularity of practice of these poses, you'll find more openness in the joints of your legs and strength in your lower back, and will be able to remain comfortable in meditation for longer periods of time. You can also consult your yoga teacher or physical therapist for suggestions on how to increase your mobility.

Chapter 7

Meditation, Contemplation, and Thinking

My teachers taught me about the mind using two principal techniques: meditation and contemplation. The intent of both is to understand the mind and realize where the source of our contentment lies, but they use different mental faculties:

• Meditation is training the mind in mindful awareness using mental skills such as concentration, attention, and relaxation. Meditation practice does not emphasize the use of concepts or the thinking mind.

• Contemplation, on the other hand, does use the intellect—those mental faculties that reason, analyze, reflect, and employ other aspects of what we might in general call "thinking." It could be described as "thinking skillfully."

In this book, we focus on meditation. But this doesn't mean that there's anything wrong with thinking and analyzing. They just aren't our objective when it comes to meditation.

Complementary practices

Meditation and contemplation are in fact complementary practices. The mental agility and pliability of the mind that we develop in our meditation practice, as well as the ability to remain undistracted, are useful skills when applied to contemplative practice.

Combining the two practices is like the way candlelight is used to read a book—the light must be still and bright. If the candle is still but not bright, we can't read the page. If the light is bright but flickers here and there, we can't read it either. Both stillness and brightness are needed. Similarly, to understand our mind deeply, the training of single-pointed concentration in meditation brings stillness, and the use of our contemplative intellect offers us illuminating insight.

In coming to know the mind, my teachers first taught me meditation because they emphasized the importance of single-pointed concentration and not being distracted. Once I had some degree of stability in resting in a non-distracted state, they had me alternate between meditation and contemplation. In a 40-minute session, for example, they suggested I meditate for the first half on my breath, or follow the other practices we have covered in this book. And then, for the next half of the session, remaining in the same meditation posture, I used the calm and collected mind to think about a question or topic. Some questions were more about the process of inquiry rather than arriving at a specific answer, such as "Where do thoughts come from, abide, and dissolve to?" or "Where is my mind located?" or "What is awareness?" I would sit for 20 minutes or so and contemplate the question, using the rope of mindfulness to rein my mind back to the topic as necessary. Then, at the conclusion of the meditation and contemplation practice, I would relax my mind completely and rest for short while, and then dedicate whatever virtue or understanding had arisen to the benefit of others.

Contemplating our meditation practice

One practical way to contemplate our meditation practice is to assess our efforts and any benefits derived from them. For example, we might contemplate the following questions, taking a frank look at our mind, attitude, and actions:

- Am I less distracted now, in meditation and in life, than before I started meditating?

- Can I stay focused on my meditation object for a longer duration before I move off into a thought loop?

- Do I feel more at ease throughout the day if I meditate in the morning?

- Am I less reactive today, in meditation and in daily life, than before I started meditating?

- Do I remain angry and upset for shorter periods now than before I started meditating?

- Can I observe sights, sounds and situations that previously aroused annoyance or displeasure with open awareness, free of my habitual reactions?

You can be creative with the questions you ponder. But you may need to be careful not to indulge the habit of self-criticism that sometimes comes when we look inwardly and think about ourselves. It is important not to criticize ourselves for anything that we may discover in our contemplation. At the same time, honestly assessing our practice is integral to the path of introspection.

One last suggestion on how to enhance your understanding of meditation by using contemplation is to write in your meditation journal. Putting pen to paper often helps clarify thinking. After you contemplate the questions above, or others that you find important, try writing down your insights in your meditation journal.

Expanding into the ever-changing present

The next meditation we'll practice is known as *Spacious Out-breath*. It is unlike our previous meditation practice in that the object that we rest our attention upon is not as defined as, for example, the breath, or sensations, or even sound. While our previous meditations tended to refine our concentration and attention, Spacious Out-breath promotes a greater sense of relaxation, even while we are being attentive.

The practice allows our awareness to mingle with the spacious gap at the end of our exhalation and can give us a glimpse into the profound state of awareness that is free of concepts. This is not, however, a practice of spacing out. Rather, we are abiding with an expanded sense of awareness, even though there isn't a "thing" upon which we fix our focus.

When we practice like this, we may have a sense that our awareness is unbound, even limitless. We might also experience how, when thinking begins, our awareness constricts tightly around a thought. In this sense, we can see how our thinking binds us, and how any panoramic awareness of the present moment is lost when we do it.

One of the effects of the practice of Spacious Out-breath is a kind of useful detachment from those things and situations around us that usually provoke anger, jealousy or negative emotions in us. This detachment arises when the power that thoughts, emotions, and external stimulation have over us wanes. The alternative is to be ruled by our thoughts or situations, or our reactions to them, which will only result in repeated cycles of dissatisfaction.

Detachment doesn't mean becoming uncaring, disconnected, or numb. Quite the contrary—it allows us to see our mind and our ever-changing world with clarity and have the discernment to act with compassion for others and for ourselves.

The practice of Spacious Out-breath tends to have a deeply calming effect on body and mind, and sometimes we can drift into a sleepy, lethargic, or sluggish state during it. We aim to be always fine-tuning our practice to balance attentiveness with relaxation, but for some individuals, a common obstacle to their meditation practice is feeling drowsy, and Spacious Out-breath is so relaxing that people sometimes fall asleep. So here are some suggestions you can use if your mind becomes drowsy. These can be used for this meditation practice or any other time you are feeling sleepy in your practice.

Top tips for avoiding drowsiness in meditation

- ❖ Straighten your spine and revive your physical posture.

- ❖ If you are feeling warm, try opening your underarms to ventilate and cool yourself.

- ❖ Let fresh air into the room to cool the temperature.

❖ Meditate with your eyes open, resting them in a downward gaze and looking into space, rather than closing them.

❖ Meditate before you take your meal.

❖ Be sure you are getting enough sleep.

❖ And finally, there's no problem in having a nice cup of tea or coffee before you meditate!

Guided meditation: Spacious out-breath

Find a comfortable seated posture on the floor or in a chair, or perhaps lie down if you have pain in some part of your body. Arrange your body so that your foundation is steady and grounded. Allow your spine to be comfortably elongated and tuck your chin under slightly. Cast your gaze downwards if your eyes are open, or gently close them. Relax completely all the muscles of your face and shoulders, and let your belly be loose and not holding any tension at all.

To establish a motivation for today's practice, perhaps you can think:

> *May today's meditation practice generate an open heart and clarity of mind, so that I can interact with my family, my community, and beyond in a mindful and compassionate way.*

Take two or three deep breaths—full inhalations into your chest and up to your collarbones, and then relaxing exhalations.

Having arranged your body in a comfortable stillness, bring your mind into your body. Feel its steadiness and motionlessness. For a few minutes, allow your attention to hover within and around your body and simply feel the most prominent sensations. Relax deeply.

Then gently turn your attention to your breath. Locate your breath wherever you feel it most strongly—maybe around your nostrils, in your chest, or in your belly. Just rest your attention there.

Feel the rising inhalation of your breath. And watch the descending exhalation.

Notice the texture of your breath, and if it is long or short. However it is, allow it to come and go naturally as you maintain a witnessing mode of attention.

Continue to relax your body while noticing your breath ... breathing in, breathing out. Balance your attentive effort with ease.

Next, while keeping your body completely still, pay attention to the end of the exhalation, and, in particular, to the gap that opens momentarily before you breathe in. You don't have to hold your breath or breathe out more strongly or manipulate your breath in some other way, just notice the slight pause, the moment, as the out-breath moves into space.

Rest in the spacious out-breath and then, as you breathe in, you can follow the inhalation ... and then once again merge your awareness with the spacious out-breath.

When your awareness rides your breath outwardly into that space, there's no need to do anything. Just abide there in space. And, as long as you are abiding in that gap, spacious and alert, remain there.

There may be some awareness of sound, or thoughts, or happenings around you, but just remain open.

Body still. Breath is natural. Mind is relaxed and attentive.

Continue to explore the spacious out-breath.

Be mindful to breathe naturally. Allow your breath to come and go, like a vast ocean that ebbs and flows.

When you start to think or get distracted, gently bring your attention back to your breath. Watch it come and go a few times, in and out, and then on an out-breath, again, rest in the spacious gap at the end of the breath.

Practice like this for the next 10–15 minutes.

As you do so, it's important not to try to block or suppress anything. The world around you can arise and pass, and thoughts too can come and go, but remain following your breath and then repeatedly resting in the spacious gap at the end of the out-breath.

To conclude your practice, on an out-breath, release any mental effort of focusing on the breath, and completely relax in silent stillness for a minute or so.

And to bring your meditation practice to an auspicious close, perhaps you can think:

> *Through my meditation practice today, may I gather the needed strength and clarity to shine more compassion and love into the world.*

Go outside!

I think it is significant that when we look at the life of great spiritual masters, we often see that they had profound insights while out of doors. When we read their biographies, we find that so many of them found solace, inspiration, and spiritual insights when they were in mountains, deserts, and forests.

Bring to mind for a moment the saints, yogis, and spiritual masters who have inspired you. I think of Saint Francis of Assisi walking barefoot in the woodlands of Umbria, or Sri Ramana Maharshi meditating in caves on Mount Arunachala, or the Zen monk Han Shan carving his poems into stone in the mountains he wandered through in eastern China.

I met one Buddhist monk in eastern Tibet who had taken a vow never to take a meal or sleep under a roof—he said it was to cultivate non-attachment to food and a home so he wouldn't be distracted from meditating! He had wandered in the mountains and lived in a simple pop-up canvas tent or in caves for his whole adult life. People who respected this monk told me that he "chose clouds as his clothes, and meditation as his sustenance."

Consider for a moment those individuals who have inspired you and where they went to meditate, to contemplate, to look deeply into themselves. Perhaps write about one of them in your meditation journal. Most likely they didn't find their inspiration inside a monastery, temple, church, or mosque, but rather in the wilderness, with the wide sky above them.

Henry David Thoreau discovered this and wrote, "I went to the woods because I wished to live deliberatively, to front only the essential facts of life, and see if I could not learn what it had to teach, and not, when I came to die, discovered that I had not lived."

Indeed, four of the most significant moments in the life of the Buddha happened under trees—his birth, his awakening, his first teaching (and many afterwards), and his passing. He suggested many times to his disciples that an ideal location for meditation was in the forest.

The saints of the past lived at a different pace than we do today and weren't inundated with the sensory stimulation of the modern world. Still, we have a choice, though it may take some self-discipline not to be continually distracted by all the stimulation.

This is precisely why getting outside is so important. We all know the rejuvenating effect and the deep rest that come from just taking a walk in the park or hiking by a river. So, why not engage in meditation beyond the comfort of our living room or meditation shrine? The simplicity of being in the natural world with open air and running water and feeling the dirt beneath our feet can be healing medicine for the mind.

Coupled with the invigorating effects of being out of doors, it is of critical importance to unplug from our computer screens and smartphones for a period of time each day—or longer! If our intention in meditation is to develop a panoramic vision externally and internally, then we must allow that to unfold from within. Screens, emails, and social media commandeer our awareness, constrict our attention, and sap our vitality. Try leaving your smartphone at home and go outside.

As for a meditation practice outside, you can engage in any of the practices in this book. In addition, let me suggest two objects upon which to rest your attention.

The sky

First, try using the sky as an object of meditation. As you have already learned, first assume your meditation posture, either seated or lying down, and after calming the body and mind with scanning the body or breathing meditation, move your attention toward the sky. Gaze into the boundless sky that has no edges. Merge your awareness with the vastness of the sky.

Of course you may drift into a thought loop, or perhaps begin to fade away or kind of space out. When this happens, revive your meditation and return to the merging of your awareness with the sky.

The space between

A second object to use for your meditation practice, especially if you are sitting in your garden or in a forest, is the space between leaves, or perhaps the space between trees.

Our habit is to look at an object, like a tree or flower. But here we allow our awareness to merge into the space or the gaps between them. It may be that you rest your attention in the space between you and the trees in front of you.

I received this meditation practice from a Native American medicine man on a park bench in Wyoming. He told me:

> *Train to see what is between us and the tree. Don't focus on the twigs themselves, but slide your mind around the branches. Don't pay attention to the flickering foliage, but look at the space between the leaves. That space is where we meet our maker, and is pregnant with possibility. Anything can arise there.*
>
> *That space is the mother of the tree; it is the mother of you and of me.*

Remember that if you can begin and close your meditation practice with a brief intention and dedication, it makes your practice all the more powerful.

Finding space in life

You may have experienced in your meditation practice how there is sometimes a gap, or a space, between stimulation—a sound, sight, or thought—and your response to that stimulation. It is a moment when you haven't reacted and remain completely present, relaxed, and aware. This moment or gap is very instructive.

Often our reactions seem automatic. We don't even recognize the moment between stimulation and response. But in meditation we can practice resting in this gap with relaxed awareness, rather than being pulled in one direction by our attachment or pushed in another by our aversion. Recognizing that there is this gap, and then repeatedly familiarizing ourselves with it, becomes a precious moment, because in this space lies our power to choose our response, or to choose not to respond at all.

The next meditation practice is known as *Resting in the Space between Thoughts*. The practice is to rest our awareness in the gap at the conclusion of one thought before another thought has formed. Some thoughts are quick and snappy, while others linger in the mind. Whatever the case, when one thought has ceased and before another has arisen, in that space, that gap, we can allow our attention to rest. Our awareness is poured into that space, like water being poured into water, and we can explore that moment deeply. Inevitably, another thought will arise at some point, and so the practice continues.

It may be that when we explore the space after one thought has ceased, when we abide in the gap, no other thoughts arise for a while. If this happens, we can allow our awareness to expand and abide in its natural state.

Resting in the space between thoughts can become a practice of not "doing" anything at all, except resting the mind in its natural, expansive, relaxed state. This kind of meditation practice is indeed a unique time, because of this "not doing." We know that our mind is always doing something—always thinking something, continually occupied with planning and strategizing. If we aren't looking at our friends' latest Facebook post or newsfeeds on our smartphones or iPads, our mind is being lured by advertisements on the radio, TV, or in magazines. But when we rest our awareness in its natural state in the gap between thoughts, mental fixations lose their purchase and get no traction. It is as if our mind has been wound up tighter and tighter and is finally released, like a snake uncoiling itself.

There is a beautiful example that nearly every one of my Tibetan Buddhist meditation teachers has used to describe the effect of this practice. It involves the imagery of a mountain stream. At some point in a stream's journey, the water flows into a clear and transparent pool. If you were to put your hand in the pool and stir the water, sediment from the bottom would rise and cloud the water. But if you were to let the water be and not stir it, the sand would settle to the bottom and the pool would return to being clear.

The clarity of the pool of water is like the natural resting-place of awareness—crystal-clear and pristine. But our continually chasing after thoughts and indulging our habitual responses alters the mind, stirring and clouding our awareness in such way that its natural clarity is obscured. Resting in the space between thoughts allows what is veiling our awareness to settle, and what emerges is our unaltered clarity and intelligence.

Guided meditation: Resting in the space between thoughts

Assume your relaxed meditation posture on the floor or in a chair, or lie down. Situate your body so that your spine maintains its natural comfortable curve as you pull your shoulders back, relax your face completely, and allow your belly to be loose and not holding any tension. Let your eyes be very relaxed, either open or closed, and not darting here and there.

Feel the steadiness of your feet, legs and hips. And rest your body in stillness.

Take a few deep breaths, inhaling all the way up to your collarbones and relaxing into a deep exhalation. Then let your breath return to its natural ebb and flow.

Turn your attention to your body as it sits motionless. Just notice how it feels right now. Feel the tactile sensations for a few moments.

Then take in the sounds around you. Again, just notice them for a few moments—there's no need to think about them or do anything except witness them.

Then observe whatever visual stimulation you see. Whether your eyes are open or closed, just notice whatever shapes, colors, lightness, or darkness you see.

Then note the tastes on your palette and whatever scents are around you.

Upon noticing something with your five senses, just let it be as it comes and goes around you.

Then turn your attention to the space of your mind. In a very relaxed manner, look at the space where thoughts, emotions, and mental images move. Observe whatever is there. There's no need to think about any of the thoughts or try to stop thoughts from arising.

When a thought occurs, watch its course. Thoughts tend to arise, remain in the space of our awareness for some time, and then dissolve. Watch this arising and dissolution.

And as you watch the arising and dissolution of thoughts, notice the space at the end of a thought before another thought begins. Look into that space, that gap.

While remaining very relaxed and very alert, allow your awareness to pervade that space completely. Remain there for however long you abide undistracted. Mingle your awareness with that space like water being poured into water.

Inevitably, another thought will arise, or you will follow a thought and begin thinking. No problem. When this happens, release the thinking, relax and return to the witness mode of bare attention, watching the arising and dissolution of thoughts, and then dive into the gap at the end of a thought, before another thought occurs. Rest there.

The gap between thoughts may be momentary, or it may last longer. It doesn't matter. Repeatedly return to and explore the space between thoughts.

If you become drowsy or your mind sinks in some manner, revive your meditation by sitting up straight, or try meditating with your eyes open.

Continue to watch the space of the mind and rest in the gap between thoughts.

A pool of water, if you don't stir it, becomes clear. Similarly, the mind, left unaltered, finds its natural clarity.

After 15 or 20 minutes of meditation, while keeping your body very still, release any effort to meditate, and rest in silent stillness for a few minutes.

You may dedicate your practice by thinking:

> *Through my practice of meditation, may I find space in my heart to care for all other beings.*

Chapter 8

Focus, Friends, and Teachers

As we bring meditation into our life, there will inevitably be challenges. I want to offer a bit of advice on how to meet those challenges by maintaining our focus, relying upon spiritual friends, and studying (or not) with a teacher.

Focus

Our purpose in meditation is to understand our mind and perception and to work skillfully with our reactions so that we engage our world with compassion and kindness for others and ourselves.

So, stay focused on understanding your mind. This means being responsible for your own inner development. To use the wise words from the hardworking folks from my home town, "Take part in your own rescue!"

Taking part in your own rescue requires returning again and again, with mindful awareness, to what does the rescuing—the mind. Take care of your mind and it will take care of you!

Inspire and support your meditation practice. There's no short supply of books on meditation, but be discerning in what material you choose. Read widely and inform yourself about your own and others' traditions, but for your practice, zero in on your own path and walk that with consistency.

Video and audio downloads, including apps of guided meditation practices, are an excellent resource—use these if they work for you. However, I remind you that meditation practice ought not to become dependent upon noise-cancelling earphones, a meditation pod, or having somebody lead you with verbal cues in class or from an app. These are all excellent supports, especially as you learn methods and techniques, but you should be careful that your meditation practice doesn't become dependent upon them.

Spiritual friends

Cultivate deep and honest friendships along your journey through meditation with individuals who respect you. These kinds of individuals are precious. We might call them "spiritual friends." Find people with whom you can share your aspirations, difficulties, and experiences.

Because we are often blind to our own missteps on the path of meditation or spiritual endeavors, or because our ego hijacks the loftiest of aspirations, we can rely on spiritual friends to point out deviations from the path, provide a reality check, and correct our course. At the same time, it is important not to navel-gaze too much with solemnity and weight. Spiritual friends are wonderful in releasing humor, exuberance, and zest for life.

The Buddha spoke often about the value of wise mentors and admirable friends in helping guide us along the spiritual path. In the *Half of the Holy Life Discourse* (*Upaddha Sutta*), his close disciple Ananda asks him whether having spiritual friends and camaraderie is "half of the holy life." The Buddha responds, "Don't say that, Ananda. Spiritual friendship and admirable companionship are actually the whole of the holy life. When a monk has admirable people as friends, companions, and comrades, he can be expected to develop and pursue the noble path [to awakening]."

Teachers

If circumstances arise where you meet a fully qualified teacher, consider studying regularly with them. This is, however, a huge step and one that should be carefully thought through. How do you know if a teacher is fully qualified? You can't know completely in the beginning, but it is acceptable to use your critical eye to judge their words and actions, as well as their close students' behavior, before making the decision to commit yourself.

Every teacher, guide, or guru you meet will have their own hang-ups, stories, and confusion, and if they aren't transparent about that confusion, I suggest you look elsewhere. Authentic teachers point the way; they are not the path itself.

Common sense also indicates that a teacher must be able to explain their teachings step by step, understand the consequences of their practices and offer their teachings with compassion and not to bolster their ego (or bank account). They should also not disparage others.

I will offer a cautionary note about teachers, because the spiritual and meditation market-place is packed these days with so-called teachers, guides, gurus, swamis, yogis, and many who have extraordinary titles indicating nothing less than a saint. *Caveat emptor*!

Often it is recommended that students feel a "connection" with a teacher, but this feeling is usually based on emotion, which is precarious at best. Charisma, humor, magnetism, charm, and eloquence may be qualities that an individual possesses, but shouldn't be the reasons we chose to study with them. Be careful and wise about selecting a teacher or guide.

Top red flags

The following behaviors and attitudes should be red flags that steer us away from so-called teachers:

- ✦ speaking of their own awakening, enlightenment or spiritual powers

- ✦ being unwilling to receive criticism of their personal behavior or teachings

- ✦ setting up a hierarchy of access to them

- ✦ displaying authoritarian behavior with no accountability

- ✦ acting contrary to what they teach or tell their students

- ✦ taking credit for the effects of others' efforts in meditation

- ✦ living opulently

- ✦ demanding that the focus of their students' attention is on them rather than their teachings

- ✦ having sexual relations with their students

Top green lights

The baseline I look for in teachers whose methods I rely upon are:

- ✦ being wise and experienced in what they teach

- ✦ being emotionally stable in their behavior

- ✦ being unpretentious in their actions

- ✦ being compassionate with their students

- ✦ being kind to everyone

I wish you well on your path of meditation, and may the auspicious conditions of sustained mental focus, spiritual friends, and wise teachers be present along the journey.

Make a Plan for Your Meditation Practice

Well done on working your way through *Meditation: Coming to Know Your Mind* and the various meditation practices presented in each chapter! Developing your meditation practice requires diligence and perseverance, and isn't always a smooth journey. But with a steady and relaxed resolve, day by day, you can peel back the layers to understand who you are at your deepest core. Congratulations and please take a moment to rejoice in your efforts!

Some of the meditation practices in this book may have worked better for you than others. Some have perhaps benefitted you in specific situations in life, while others may not have resonated so much with you. Identify what has worked, and note it down in your meditation journal.

Trust your experience of what has worked, and what hasn't been useful. As the wonderful meditation teacher Sharon Salzberg said, "The greatest source of faith or confidence in the path is one's own experience of the power of one's own mind or inherent goodness, which meditation can readily provide."

Continue with enthusiasm to work with the meditation techniques that you find most helpful right now. It is more useful to practice one method consistently day after day, year after year, than to be familiar with dozens of techniques but never really dive deeply into them.

You have some experience with meditating at this point. You have recognized positive mental habits that contribute to your contentment and not-so-helpful mental habits, including where you encounter resistance to meditating. You are also probably more aware of what in your life supports the development of your meditation practice and what doesn't.

So now is the time to make a plan for your meditation practice. Maybe your plan will be for the next month, or perhaps longer, even six months. Whatever the duration, take some time to consider what is helpful for your daily meditation practice and what you might want to relinquish. Is what you eat and drink supportive to meditation? What about the time of your meals? Is what you read, listen to, or watch helpful to calming your body and mind before you meditate? Perhaps consider the people you spend time with, or the activities you do in your spare time, and reflect on whether they are supportive or not to your meditation practice.

For example, many people have told me that they want to meditate every day before they go to work, but never have quite enough time before they rush out of the door. Rather than trying to squeeze more in, or cutting things out from their morning, which is not always possible with families and commutes, I recommend examining what they are usually doing during the evening. If they go to bed an hour or even 30 minutes earlier than usual, they can wake up earlier and have ample time for meditation. This may mean less Netflix watching, or time online, but inevitably we have to make such choices.

Another example comes from those people who have told me they want to meditate at night, but always fall asleep when they sit to practice. Again, I encourage them to look at supportive circumstances and suggest meditating earlier in the evening, before they have their meal, rather than making meditation the last thing they do before bedtime. We know that a belly full of food makes for a groggy meditation session.

There are many small but significant supportive circumstances that can contribute to establishing a daily meditation practice. So, make a plan, write it down, adjust it when you need to, and continue day by day with a balance of eagerness and calmness.

Consistency is the key

There will be seemingly good days and bad days with your meditation practice. You may have some resistance to meditating too. Resistance and similar mental habits that prevent us from moving deeply into our mind are not uncommon, but can be a real obstacle to meditation practice.

Resistance is like a huge bolder of granite. If we want to break it open, but the only tool we have is water, how do we crack it? If the water drips slowly, day after day, month after month, eventually the constancy of the drip will crack the toughest of granite.

Similarly, our humble, consistent daily meditation practice can crack the most solidified of our mental habits. As the Buddha said in *The Path* (*Maggavagga*), "Wisdom springs from meditation; without meditation wisdom wanes. Having known these two paths of progress and decline, let a woman or man so conduct themselves that their wisdom may increase."

When I first started meditating in Nepal 23 years ago, I remember seeing a sign at a retreat center. It read: "The Continuity of Practice is the Secret of Success." At the time I didn't appreciate fully what it meant. Now I do.

I've engaged in intense periods of retreat, spending over 10 hours a day seated in meditation for weeks on end. I've had busy periods in my life in Washington, DC, New York, and Kathmandu, where I've struggled to find a few minutes in the morning to meditate before I rushed off to my work. And there have been sweet spots where my hour-long meditation practice in the morning has flowed directly into my daily duties. As that sign told me so many years ago, it is in the continuity of meditation practice, in the consistency, that I've discovered the benefits to my body, to my mind, and to my heart.

There will be periods of time when you need to take care of others, work long hours, or endure stress—and these are the times when meditation is of the greatest benefit. So, strive on with enthusiasm.

The ripple effect

We began our practice of meditation in this book with an intention. Our intention was to develop clarity of mind and softness of heart so that we might more skillfully benefit others in our family, community and well beyond. We repeatedly prompted ourselves with this intention before each meditation practice. Then we meditated without grasping for results—we just practiced. And after meditating, we dedicated the power and virtue of our practice so that any benefit might ripple into the world to bring deep contentment and alleviate suffering for others. In the same manner that we began and concluded each meditation session, so we will end this book with a dedication so that our efforts will continue to expand.

Before offering a concluding dedication, with a deep bow of respect I want to commend you again for all the energy, effort, and determination that you have put forth in order to develop and sustain your meditation practice.

As you take the next steps on your path of meditation, know that deep within you resides all the wisdom and compassion that you'll ever need. This is fundamental to your being—it is who you are at the deepest level.

While anxiety, fear, or angst may at times temporarily veil your awareness of these abiding strengths, know that they are always accessible. Your meditation practice will pull back the veils. As they are removed, what is revealed will be wise and caring discernment.

Trust yourself as this discernment emerges. And then, confidently, go into the world with unbounded kindness and love to share with others.

Through the truth and strength of our meditation practice,

May wisdom and compassion spring forth from our being,

So that we may quickly alleviate suffering for all beings

And spread contentment, love, and joy throughout the world.

Further Reading

Bhikkhu Bodhi, *In the Buddha's Words*, Wisdom Publications, 2005

Tara Brach, *Radical Acceptance*, Bantam Dell, 2003

Bhikkhu Buddhadasa, *Mindfulness with Breathing*, Wisdom Publications, 1988

Pema Chödrön, *When Things Fall Apart*, Shambhala Publications, 1997

——, *How to Meditate*, Sounds True, 2013

The Dalai Lama, *Ethics for a New Millennium*, Riverhead Books, 1999

——, *Essence of the Heart Sutra*, Wisdom Publications, 2002

Joseph Goldstein, *The Experience of Insight*, Shambhala Publications, 1976

Michaela Haas, *Dakini Power*, Snow Lion, 2013

Thich Nhat Hanh, *The Miracle of Mindfulness*, Beacon Press, 1975

——, *Old Path White Clouds*, Parallax Press, 1991

Jon Kabat-Zinn, *Wherever You Go, There You Are*, Hyperion, 1994

Jack Kornfield, *Meditation for Beginners*, Bantam, 2005

Mattieu Ricard, *Why Meditate?*, NiL Editions, Paris, 2008; Hay House, 2010

Tenzin Wangyal Rinpoche, *The True Source of Healing*, Hay House, 2015

Sharon Salzberg, *Real Happiness*, Workman Publishing Company, 2010

——, *Real Love*, Flatiron Books, 2017

Chögyam Trungpa, *Cutting Through Spiritual Materialism*, Shambhala Publications, 1973

——, *Meditation in Action*, Shambhala Publications, 2010

B. Alan Wallace, *The Attention Revolution*, Wisdom Publications, 2006

——, *Minding Closely*, Snow Lion Publications, 2011

Index

A

acceptance 8

adept's pose (*Siddhasana*) 132

altruism 62–3

Ananda 157

appearances 76, 114–15, 116
    identification with 114–15

Asanga 40, 41, 61

attention 58–9
    and body scanning *see* body scanning
    on the breath *see* breath
    concentration *see* concentration
    and distractions *see* distractions
    and posture 27

auditory consciousness 121

awareness 2, 6, 8, 44, 58, 74–7
    and cognizance 76–7, 113
    discerning reality with 51–66

extracting us from seventh consciousness 126–7

and illumination 74–6

pure awareness
    and the first six consciousnesses 123

resting in 148–53

returning to pure awareness 77, 127

self-empowerment through 116–19

seventh consciousness
    and the defilement of pure awareness 124–5

see also consciousnesses, eight; mindfulness

B

Baddhakonasan (Cobbler's pose) 133

bliss 87–9

body scanning
  connecting body and
    mind through 18–23
  guided meditation
    30–33
  spontaneous/informal
    98
breath
  breathing meditation
    63–6, 98, 146
  guided meditations
    the breath as our
      companion 54–6
    discovering the breath
      36–8
    relaxed and alert with
      the breath 63–6
    spacious out-breath
      141–3
  as a meditation support
    34–6, 54–6
  spacious out-breath
    139–43
Buddha 5, 7, 52, 63, 79–80,
    145, 157
  Half of the Holy Life
    Discourse 157
  Root Sequence Discourse
    81

C
clarity 87–9
Cobbler's pose
    (Baddhakonasan)
    133
cognizance 76–7, 113
  see also awareness

comfort 17, 131–4
  becoming too comfortable
    in meditation practice
    93–4
compassion 3, 63, 79–80,
    155
concentration 6, 8, 12, 51
  and distraction see
    distractions
consciousnesses, eight
    120–27
  first to fifth, and the
    physical world 120–21
  sixth, and the mental
    world 121–3
  seventh, and the
    defilement of pure
    awareness 124–5, 127
  eighth, and the storing of
    habits 125–7
contemplation 135–8
contentment 3–4, 114, 165
Coward, Noël 126–7

D
Dalai Lama 67, 129–30
defiling consciousness
    124–5, 127
detachment 139–40
discernment 4, 68, 140, 166
  discerning reality with
    awareness 51–66
distractions 39–43
  dealing with strong
    emotions and
    'experiences' during
    meditation 85–7, 94

Eight Consciousnesses
    map of 120–27
    mindfulness as antidote
        to 40–41, 61–2 *see also*
        mindfulness
    releasing, relaxing, and
        returning from 41–3
    self-criticism over 43–4
    transforming distraction
        into meditation
        78–80
drink 106–7
    guided meditation on
        drinking tea 108–9
drowsiness 140–41

E
eating 106–7
    guided meditation 110–11
ego 125, 157, 158
Eight Consciousnesses
    see consciousnesses,
    eight
Eliot, T.S. 9
emotional experiences
        during meditation
        85–7, 94
empathy 62–3
ethical framework for
        meditation 12–15,
        62–3, 155
eyes 23–4

F
Francis of Assisi 144
friends, spiritual 156–7

G
Goenka, S.N xvii
guided meditation
    body scanning 30–33
    on the breath
        the breath as our
            companion 54–6
        discovering the breath
            36–8
        relaxed and alert with
            the breath 63–6
        spacious out-breath
            141–3
    drinking tea 108–9
    eating 110–11
    'mind' 117–19
    resting in the space
        between thoughts
        150–53
    on the senses
        all five senses 82–5
        hearing, and sound
            71–3
    walking 101–3
gustatory consciousness
    121

H
habit
    habitual responses of
        seventh consciousness
        124–5, 127
    storehouse 125–7
    thinking 70
Han Shan 144
Hanh, Thich Nhat 78–9, 99,
        100, 109

hearing *see* sound and hearing
Hero's pose (*Virasana*) 133

I
ignorance 115
illumination 74–6
inquiry 8

J
journals 10, 48, 131, 161

K
Kabat-Zinn, Jon 60–61

L
lotus position (*Padmasana*) 132

M
Malasana (squat pose) 134
meditation
    avoiding drowsiness in 140–41
    awakening to present moment with 52–3 *see also* present moment
    becoming too comfortable in 93–4
    beginning 9–15
    being kind to ourselves in 43–5
    benefits of 3–4, 6–7, 8
    bliss, clarity and no-thought during 87–9
    consistency as key to 163–5
    and contemplation 135–8
    developing an interest in 95–7
    discernment through *see* discernment
    emotional experiences during 85–7, 94
    eyes in 23–4
    food, drink and 106–11
    integration into everyday life 95–111
    introductory overview 1–8
    journals 10, 48, 131, 161
    moral/ethical framework for 12–15, 62–3, 155
    motivation 3–4, 11, 14–15, 45
    outdoor 144–7 *see also* walking meditation
    pain during 22–3, 89–92
    planning your practice 161–3
    posture *see* posture
    practices and techniques
        body scanning *see* body scanning
        with the breath *see* breath
        cultivating the mind through 4–5
        cultivating stillness through 17–49, 56–7

dealing with
distractions *see*
distractions
discerning reality with
51–66
guided meditation *see*
guided meditation
keeping practice close
to the heart 46
length of sessions
45–6
letting go before
sleeping 105–6
making a commitment
47–8
and mindfulness *see*
mindfulness
motivation and
dedication 14–15
opening completely to
our world through
67–94
rejoicing at end of
sessions 49
ripple effect of
practice 165
using our senses
see senses and
sensations
tips for establishing a
daily practice
45–9
triggering strong
emotions and
'experiences'
85–7
Vipassana xvii, 21–3,
86–7

walking *see* walking
meditation
working within our
mind 113–31
as a process and vehicle
2–3, 53
resistance to 21, 162,
163–4
on the sky 146–7
and sleep *see* sleep
space/location 11, 92–3,
144–8
spontaneous and informal
97–9
support 156–60
teacher selection 157–9
tools 6, 8 *see
also* awareness;
concentration;
mindfulness;
spaciousness
mental consciousness 121–3
mental narratives 20
mindfulness 12, 60–62
abiding 62
as antidote to distraction
40–41, 61–2
guided meditation, 'mind'
117–19
leading to compassion
62–3, 79–80, 155
pain management
through 91
and the present moment
see present moment
prospective 62
and sleep 104–6
see also awareness

mobility training 131
moral framework for
        meditation 12–15,
        62–3, 155
motivation 3–4, 11, 14–15, 45

N
no-thought 87–9

O
olfactory consciousness 121
outdoor meditation 144–7
        see also walking
        meditation

P
Padmasana (lotus position)
        132
pain 22–3, 89–92
Pascal, Blaise 57–8
posture 11, 23–9, 57, 131–4
        Adept's 132
        alertness in 23
        Cobbler's 133
        and comfort 17, 131–4
        flexibility, mobility and
                131–4
        and gaze 24
        Hero's 133
        lotus 132
        seven-point 26
        sitting 25, 132–3
        squat 134
        supine 27–9
present moment 2, 52–3, 91

expanding into ever-
        changing present
        139–43
purifying the mind 126

R
Ramana Maharshi 144
reality
        and appearance 76,
                114–15
        discernment of 51–66
rejoicing 49
resistance 21, 162, 163–4
resting in the space between
        thoughts 118–19,
        148–53
rope/snake illusion 115

S
Salzberg, Sharon 161–2
scent 81
        olfactory consciousness
                121
senses and sensations
        body scanning for
                sensations *see* body
                scanning
        consciousnesses of
                120–21
        guided meditations
                on all five senses
                        82–5
                on hearing and sound
                        71–3
        just feeling the sensation
                80, 91–2, 118

meditating on objects of
our five senses 68–73,
82–5
opening to all five senses
80–85
Siddhasana (adept's pose)
132
sight 81, 118
visual consciousness 121
silence 56, 57–8
sky 146–7
sleep
letting go before sleeping
105–6
quality 103–5
Snyder, Gary 128–30
sound and hearing 80, 118
auditory consciousness
121
guided meditation 71–3
spaciousness 6, 8, 59
spacious out-breath
139–43
spiritual friends 156–7
squat pose (*Malasana*) 134
stillness
cultivating 17–49, 56–7
resting in 118
storehouse consciousness
125–7
subconscious 125–7

T
tactile consciousness 121
taste 81, 118
gustatory consciousness
121

tea drinking, guided
meditation 108–9
teacher selection 157–9
Tertön Sogyal 128
thinking
attachment and aversion
to thoughts 70
and being kind to
ourselves 43–5
blocking sight of reality
67–8
and contemplation 135–8
distracting thoughts
see distractions
habit 70
no-thought 87–9
and recalling ourselves
see mindfulness
resting in the space
between thoughts
118–19, 148–53
seventh consciousness
and the defilement of
pure awareness 124–5
Thoreau, Henry David 145
touch 102, 121

V
Vipassana meditation xvii,
21–3, 86–7
Virasana (Hero's pose) 133
visual consciousness 121

W
walking meditation 99–100
guided 101–3
Wallace, B. Alan 124

ABOUT THE AUTHOR

Matteo Pistono is a writer and meditation and *pranayama* teacher. His books include *In the Shadow of the Buddha: One Man's Journey of Discovery in Tibet* (Dutton Penguin, 2011) and *Fearless in Tibet: The Life of the Mystic Tertön Sogyal* (Hay House 2014). Pistono's writings and photographs about Tibetan, Himalayan, and South East Asian cultural, political, and spiritual landscapes have also appeared in the *Washington Post*, the BBC's In Pictures, *Men's Journal*, *Kyoto Journal*, and *HIMAL South Asia*.

Pistono was born and raised in Wyoming, completed an undergraduate degree in anthropology at the University of Wyoming, and in 1997 obtained a Master of Arts degree in Indian philosophy from the School of Oriental and African Studies, University of London.

After working with the Smithsonian Institution in Washington, DC, on Tibetan cultural programs, Pistono lived and traveled throughout the Himalayas for a decade, bringing to the West graphic accounts and photos of China's human rights abuses in Tibet, which he wrote about in *In the Shadow of the Buddha*.

He sits on the Executive Council of the International Network of Engaged Buddhists.

www.matteopistono.com

Meditation
Made Easy
Online Video Course

Come to know your heart and mind in the innermost way.

Matteo Pistono's informative course will introduce you to the wonderful effects of meditation and help you to establish a regular practice to transform your life. With four hours of video lessons, guided meditations, practical exercises and a meditation journal to record your progress, this is an accessible and comprehensive introduction to meditation.

You'll learn how to:

- **Become mindful and present in every moment**
- **Develop meditation practices to calm your body and mind**
- **Transform your relationship to your thoughts**
- **Discover profound contentment and joy from within**
- **Master meditation positions, posture and breathing**

Meditation is the perfect antidote to hectic modern life.

Whether you want to relieve anxiety, improve your sleep, deal with frustration or be more present, meditation is a fantastic way to bring inner peace, emotional grounding and contentment into your life. Matteo will equip you with the knowledge and techniques you need to develop a powerful connection between your body and mind, establish a regular practice within your schedule, and meditate with calmness, comfort and confidence.

Learn more at: hayhouse.co.uk/meditation

Hay House Podcasts
Bring Fresh, Free Inspiration Each Week!

Hay House proudly offers a selection of life-changing audio content via our most popular podcasts!

Hay House Meditations Podcast

Features your favorite Hay House authors guiding you through meditations designed to help you relax and rejuvenate. Take their words into your soul and cruise through the week!

Dr. Wayne W. Dyer Podcast

Discover the timeless wisdom of Dr. Wayne W. Dyer, world-renowned spiritual teacher and affectionately known as "the father of motivation." Each week brings some of the best selections from the 10-year span of Dr. Dyer's talk show on HayHouseRadio.com.

Hay House World Summit Podcast

Over 1 million people from 217 countries and territories participate in the massive online event known as the Hay House World Summit. This podcast offers weekly mini-lessons from World Summits past as a taste of what you can hear during the annual event, which occurs each May.

Hay House Radio Podcast

Listen to some of the best moments from HayHouseRadio.com, featuring expert authors such as Dr. Christiane Northrup, Anthony William, Caroline Myss, James Van Praagh, and Doreen Virtue discussing topics such as health, self-healing, motivation, spirituality, positive psychology, and personal development.

Hay House Live Podcast

Enjoy a selection of insightful and inspiring lectures from Hay House Live, an exciting event series that features Hay House authors and leading experts in the fields of alternative health, nutrition, intuitive medicine, success, and more! Feel the electricity of our authors engaging with a live audience, and get motivated to live your best life possible!

Find Hay House podcasts on iTunes, or visit www.HayHouse.com/podcasts for more info.

HAY HOUSE

Look within

Join the conversation about latest products, events, exclusive offers and more.

f Hay House UK

🐦 @HayHouseUK

📷 @hayhouseuk

💜 healyourlife.com

We'd love to hear from you!